797,885 Books

are available to read at

Forgotten Books

www.ForgottenBooks.com

Forgotten Books' App
Available for mobile, tablet & eReader

ISBN 978-1-334-02139-8
PIBN 10704648

This book is a reproduction of an important historical work. Forgotten Books uses state-of-the-art technology to digitally reconstruct the work, preserving the original format whilst repairing imperfections present in the aged copy. In rare cases, an imperfection in the original, such as a blemish or missing page, may be replicated in our edition. We do, however, repair the vast majority of imperfections successfully; any imperfections that remain are intentionally left to preserve the state of such historical works.

Forgotten Books is a registered trademark of FB &c Ltd.
Copyright © 2015 FB &c Ltd.
FB &c Ltd, Dalton House, 60 Windsor Avenue, London, SW19 2RR.
Company number 08720141. Registered in England and Wales.

For support please visit www.forgottenbooks.com

1 MONTH OF FREE READING

at

www.ForgottenBooks.com

By purchasing this book you are eligible for one month membership to ForgottenBooks.com, giving you unlimited access to our entire collection of over 700,000 titles via our web site and mobile apps.

To claim your free month visit:
www.forgottenbooks.com/free704648

* Offer is valid for 45 days from date of purchase. Terms and conditions apply.

English
Français
Deutsche
Italiano
Español
Português

www.forgottenbooks.com

Mythology Photography **Fiction**
Fishing Christianity **Art** Cooking
Essays Buddhism Freemasonry
Medicine **Biology** Music **Ancient Egypt** Evolution Carpentry Physics
Dance Geology **Mathematics** Fitness
Shakespeare **Folklore** Yoga Marketing
Confidence Immortality Biographies
Poetry **Psychology** Witchcraft
Electronics Chemistry History **Law**
Accounting **Philosophy** Anthropology
Alchemy Drama Quantum Mechanics
Atheism Sexual Health **Ancient History**
Entrepreneurship Languages Sport
Paleontology Needlework Islam
Metaphysics Investment Archaeology
Parenting Statistics Criminology
Motivational

THE
PROVERBS OF WALES:

A COLLECTION OF WELSH PROVERBS,

WITH ENGLISH TRANSLATIONS.

COMPILED BY

T. R. ROBERTS.

"*The genius, wit, and spirit of a nation are discovered by their proverbs.*"—LORD BACON.

PENMAENMAWR : T. R. ROBERTS.

1885.

"POB DIAREB GWIR, POB COEL CELWYDD."
"EVERY PROVERB IS TRUTH, EVERY REPORT A LIE."

PREFACE.

It is a somewhat remarkable fact that, whilst collections of French, Italian, German, Spanish and Portuguese Proverbs have, within the last few years, been presented to English readers in their own language, no such collection of Welsh Proverbs has been published. It is true that in 1658 a small collection of "Old Cambrian Sayed Sawes and Adages" rendered into English was appended by James Howell to his *Lexicon Tetraglotton*, and that in the following year they were published separately in a small book of 48 pages. Very few copies, however, of Howell's collection are now extant, and as far as the compiler of the present work has been able to ascertain no further attempt was made in the same direction. That the Welsh possess a collection of Proverbs which will compare favourably with those of other nations will not be denied by those who have paid any attention to the literature of Wales.

It is felt that a few words are necessary with regard to the plan of the work. D'Israeli in his "Essay on the Philosophy of Proverbs," remarks that "the arrangement of proverbs has baffled the ingenuity "of every one of their collectors." In the present collection, the proverbs are classified under various heads, according to what is conceived to be the subject matter of each proverb; for instance, proverbs relating to *health* are arranged alphabetically under that heading. The Welsh headings are arranged in alphabetical order throughout the work, and for the convenience of English readers an index to the English headings is added at the end. It is possible that many into whose hands this collection may come would prefer the usual plan of arranging the proverbs in alphabetical order only, but it is believed that the arrangement adopted in the following pages has advantages not possessed by the plan referred to, and that thereby the value of the work as a book of reference is to some extent increased.

It is hoped that this attempt to publish in a concise and handy form an English version of these ancient Welsh maxims may not be deemed to be altogether a failure, but that it may meet with some little favour at the hands of the public.

T. R. R.

Penmaenmawr,
    North Wales,
        January 26th, 1885.

THE
PROBERBS OF WALES.

"Plant gwirionedd yw hen ddiarhebion."
"Old proverbs are the children of truth."

ACHWYN.

1. A achwyno heb achos gwneler achos iddo.
2. A gŵyn rwy ni rygwynfan.
3. Achwyn rhag achwyn rhagddo.
4. Cas ddyn a achwyno ar bob achos ar na fo gwir achos cwyno.
5. Gwae heb raid a wnel achwyn.
6. Iach rydd rhyfedd pa gŵyn.
7. Ni chŵyn ci er ei daraw âg asgwrn.
8. Ni chŵyn yr iar fod y gwalch yn glaf.
9. Trist yw cŵyn pob colledig.
10. Yr ŷch llog ni fedr achwyn.

ADFYD.

1. Adfyd a bair i rai edrych o'u deutu.
2. Adfyd a ddaw a dysg yn ei law.
3. Adfyd a ddwg wybodaeth, a gwybodaeth ddoethineb.
4. Adfyd pob hir dristwch.
5. Adfyd a phall a wnant ddyn yn gall.

COMPLAINT.

1. He who complains without cause let a cause be made for him.
2. He who complains of excess does not grieve at all.
3. To complain lest he should himself be complained of.
4. Odious is he who always complains without any cause.
5. Woe fo him who complains without any cause.
6. With health at liberty it is wonderful what complaint.
7. A dog will not complain though struck by a bone.
8. The hen will not complain that the hawk is sick.
9. Sadly does every condemned one complain.
10. The hired ox cannot complain.

ADVERSITY.

1. Adversity makes people look about them.
2. Adversity comes with instruction in its hand.
3. Adversity bringeth knowledge, and knowledge wisdom.
4. Every continuing sadness is a calamity.
5. Adversity and loss make a man wise.

6. Dirwest, a chred a gweddi, a orfydd pob caledi.
7. Drwg trallodau, gwaeth hebddynt.
8. Goreu athraw caledi.
9. Gwae a gawdd (gystuddio) Duw ac nis cred.
10. Llawer doeth dwys ei adfyd.
11. Pan fo ingaf gan ddyn ehangaf gan Dduw.
12. Trallodion yw ffyn yr ysgol sydd yn esgyn i'r nef.
13. Ymbaratoi i gyfarfod adfyd yw y ffordd nesaf at hawddfyd.
14. Yn mhob cyfyngder y mae addysg.
15. Yn yr ing goreu yw y câr.

ADDEWID.

1. Addaw mawr a rhodd fechan.
2. Addaw teg a wna ynfyd yn llawen.
3. Addaw y môr a'r mynydd.
4. Addewid gwragedd dau-eiriog.
5. Câs a addawo bobpeth ac heb gywiro dim.
6. Dyled ar bawb ei addaw (addewid.)
7. Ewyn dwfr addewid gwas,

6. Temperance, faith and prayer, will overcome every difficulty.
7. Evil are afflictions, worse without them.
8. The best teacher is adversity.
9. Woe to him whom God afflicts and who believes not.
10. Many a wise man meets with grave calamity.
11. The more difficult with man the more comprehensive with God.
12. Troubles are the steps of the ladder which ascends to heaven.
13. To prepare to meet adversity is the nearest way to happiness.
14. There is a lesson in every perplexity.
15 In distress a friend is best.

PROMISE.

1. To promise much and give little.
2. A fair promise makes the fool merry.
3. To promise the sea and mountain.
4. The promise of fickle-women.
5. Hateful is he who promises everything and fulfils nothing.
6. One's promise is a debt.
7. A youth's promise is like the froth of water.

8. Gwell nag na dau addewid.
9. Gwell nag na gau addewid.
10. Gwell nag, nag addewid ni wneir.

11. Gwell un hwda na dau addaw.
12. Hawdd addaw ond anhawdd cywiraw.
13. Llesgedd yw tori godduned (adduned.)
14. Llygad Duw ar adneu (ymrwymiad.)
15. Ni lenwir uffern eithr âg addewidion da.
16. Odid addewid a ddel.
17. Un peth yw addaw, peth arall yw cywiraw.

ADDFWYNDER.

1. Dedwydd (addfwyn) pawb wrth a'i llocho.
2. Nid mwynder ond merch.
3. Nid yn yr araf y bydd fwyaf y mwynder.
4. Nid mynych gwâr dyn chwedleugar.
5. Nid oes un gwâr heb iddo anrhydedd.
6. Y gwâr (addfwyn) a gânt barch lle bynag y byddont.
7. Yr addfwyn a geiff nawdd gan frodor ac estron,

8. A refusal is better than two promises.
9. A refusal is better than a false promise.
10. A refusal is better than a promise never to be performed.
11. Better one "take" than two promises.
12. It is easy to promise but difficult to perform.
13. To break a vow is weakness.
14. God's eye on a pledge.
15. Hell will not be filled except with fair promises.
16. The promise that is kept is rare.
17. It is one thing to promise, another to perform.

MEEKNESS.

1. All are meek to those who protect them.
2. There is no tenderness but in a woman.
3. The greatest meekness is not always in the mild.
4. A talkative man is not often meek.
5. There are none meek but that are honoured.
6. The meek shall be honoured wherever they are.
7. The meek will be protected by natives and strangers.

ADDYSG.

1. Addysg doeth ei ymbwyll.
2. Addysg ffol ei ymbrawf.
3. Addysga dy hun cyn y dysgot arall.
4. A gymmero ddysg cadwed.
5. Alwar (pwrs) llawn dysg a dawn.
6. Cadw yn graff a ddysgych.
7. Cas ddyn a ddysgo lawer ac ni wyddo ddim.
8. Cas esgob heb ddysgeidiaeth.
9. Cas plwyf heb ddysg.
10. Cas ysgolhaig heb lyfrau.
11. Deuparth bonedd yw dysg.
12. Deuparth dysg yw hyder.
13. Dysg dedwydd â gair,
    Dysg dirïaid â gwiail.
14. Dysg hyd angeu, ac angeu i'r sawl na ddysgo.
15. Dysg yn graff a welych.
16. Ef a geiff dyn ddysg o'i febyd hyd ei henaint.
17. Gnawd (naturiol) i ddysgedig lyfrgell.

EDUCATION.

1. The instruction of the wise his consideration.
2. The instruction of the fool his experience.
3. Teach thyself before teaching others.
4. He who takes learning let him keep it.
5. Learning and talent make a full purse.
6. Keep securely what thou learnest.
7. Odious is he who learns much and knows nothing.
8. Odious is a bishop without learning.
9. Odious is a parish without education.
10. Odious is a scholar without books.
11. Two-thirds of nobility is education.
12. Two-thirds of education is assurance.
13. Teach the discreet with a word,
    Teach the stubborn with rods.
14. Education until death, and death to such as will not learn.
15. Learn with quickness what thou seest.
16. Man learns from childhood to old age.
17. It is natural for the learned to have a library.

18. Goreu arf, arf dysg.
19. Goreu dysg ystyriaeth.
20. Gwell dysg na golud cyfrben (cyflawn.)
21. Gwell na llên pwyll cynhenid.
22. Heb addysg nis gellir pwyll.
23. Heb ddysg, heb ddawn.
24. Llyfr mawr, tomen fawr.
25. Mae yn rhaid i bawb dalu am ei ddysgu.
26. Ni ddysg, ni wrendy.
27. Ni wyr, ni ddysg.
28. Nid addysg heb athraw.
29. Nid doeth ni ddarlleno.
30. Nid dysg heb synwyr.
31. Nid dysg ond gair Duw.
32. Nid rhy hên neb i ddysgu.
33. Pan aned dysg daeth twyll i'n mysg,
    Pan ddysger dysg daw gwir i'n mysg.

18. The best weapon is education.
19. The best education is reflection.
20. Better education than perfect wealth.
21. Better than learning is natural talent.
22. Without education there can be no discretion.
23. Without education, without gift.
24. A great book, a great dunghill.
25. All must pay for being taught.
26. He will not learn, that will not listen.
27. He does not know, that does not learn.
28. There is no education without a teacher.
29. He is not wise who does not read.
30. There is no learning without sense.
31. There is no learning but the word of God.
32. No one is too old to learn.
33. When learning was born delusion came,
    When learning becomes learned truth will come.

AFIECHYD.

1. A fo claf efe a orwedd.
2. Afiach pob trwm galon.
3. Anaf yn ngiau, angeu yn ngwythi.
4. Astrus pob anaf.
5. Bid nych cwyn claf.
6. Bod yn glaf a marw eisys.
7. Cryd (twymyn) ar hên angeu ys dir (sicr.)
8. Gnawd i glaf ofni angeu.
9. Hawdd yw clwyfo claf.
10. Hir nych i angeu.
11. Llaw pawb ar ei anaelau (briwiau.)
12. Lle y bo y dolur y bydd y llaw.
13. Ni chêl grudd gystudd calon.
14. Ni ludd nerth afiechyd.
15. Ni wna lês gormod cystudd.
16. Nid un anian iach a chlaf.
17. Peswch sych diwedd pob nych (gwendid.)
18. Pob hir nychdod i angeu.

SICKNESS.

1. He who is sick will lie down.
2. Diseased is every heavy-hearted.
3. Disease in the nerves, death in the veins.
4. Perplexing is every deformity.
5. Languishing be the complaint of the sick.
6. To be long sick and die besides.
7. Fever to the aged is certain death.
8. It is natural for the sick to fear death.
9. It is easy to wound the sick.
10. Long pining to death.
11. Everyone's hand on his sore.
12. Where the wound is there will the hand be.
13. The cheek will not conceal the anguish of the heart.
14. Strength will not keep disease away.
15. Too much sickness does no good.
16. The healthy and the sick are not of the same disposition.
17. A dry cough is the end of every weakness.
18. Every long affliction leads to death.

19. Trech na chant cystudd calon.
20. Udgorn angeu yw peswch sych.
21. Yn mhob clwyf y mae perygl.

AFLWYDDIANT.

1. Aflwyddianus pob diriaid.
2. Esmwythaf gwaith yw methu.
3. Hwyrwaith i anffynedig.
4. Mawr toraeth aflwydd pan fyno.
5. Mawr yw toraeth yr aflwydd.
6. Mwyaf poen yw poen methiant.

19. Stronger than a hundred is the anguish of the heart.
20. A dry cough is the trumpet of death.
21. In every disease there is danger.

FAILURE.

1. Unprosperous is every wicked one.
2. The easiest work is failure.
3. A late turn to the unprosperous.
4. Great is the store of misfortune when he commands.
5. Great is the store of the unfortunate.
6. The greatest pain is the pain of failure.

AMAETHYDDIAETH.

1. Adwyog (bylchog) cae anhwsmon.
2. Beudŷ oer, ystabl gynhes.
3. Bydd fyw march a gnith wellt Mai.
4. Cas gardd heb lysiau.
5. Cas perllan heb afalau.
6. Cell maeronwr (llaethwr) ei fuarth.
7. G'nawd o egin meithrin dâs.
8. Goreu arf, arf amaethwr.
9. Goreu cloff, cloff aradr.
10. Goreu gwrthwyneb, gwrthwyneb cwys.
11. Goreu o'r geifr, y gwynion.
12. Goreu o'r haidd, y byraf.
13. Goreu o'r meirch, y mwyaf.
14. Goreu o'r moch, y tewaf.
15. Goreu un anifail, buwch.
16. Gwae oferwr yn nghynhauaf.
17. Gwell eidion gwerth nag un pryn.

AGRICULTURE.

1. Full of gaps is the field of a bad farmer.
2. A cold cowhouse, and a warm stable.
3. The steed will live that nibbles the grass of May.
4. Odious is a garden without herbs.
5. Odious is an orchard without apples.
6. The dairyman's parlour is his fold.
7. From the small shoots a rick is reared.
8. The best tool is the farmer's.
9. The best crooked thing is the crooked handle of a plough.
10. The best inversion is the inversion of the furrow.
11. The best goats, the white.
12. The best barley, the shortest.
13. The best horse, the largest.
14. The best sow, the fattest.
15. The best of all animals, the cow.
16. Woe to the idler during harvest.
17. Better a selling beast than a bought one.

18. Gwell haner hâd na haner hâf.
19. Gwlybaniaeth yn yr ôg, chwyn yn y cryman.
20. Hau ar y sych-hîn,
    Planu ar y gwlyb-hîn.
21. Hawdd medi erw anghenog.
22. Lleilai lymaid gauaf.
23. Llwm tir ni phoro dafad.
24. Mae yr ymenyn yn nghyrn y fuwch.
25. Melysaf y gwellt nesaf i'r ddaear.
26. Ni chêl drygdir ei egin.
27. Ni wna geiriau têg hau y tir.
28. Nid mynachdod maeroni (amaethyddiaeth.)
29. Pan fo culaf yr ŷch goreu fydd yn ngwaith.
30. Pum diwrnod hau, y tridiau olaf o Fawrth a dau lygad Ebrill.
31. Rhaid cael eiddo i drin tir.
32. Tra rhedo yr ôg rheded y ffraean.
33. Tra rhedo yr ôg y rhêd y ddraenglwyd.
34. Trymion gnydau, gwlyb gynhauaf.

18. Better half seed than half summer.
19. Moisture in the harrow, weeds in the reaping hook.
20. Sow in dry weather,
    Plant in wet weather.
21. It is easy to reap the acre of the poor.
22. Less and less the draught of winter.
23. Bare is the land a sheep will not graze.
24. The butter is in the cow's horns.
25. The sweeter the grass the nearer the earth.
26. Bad land will not conceal its vegetation.
27. Fair words will not sow the land.
28. Husbandry is no monkery.
29. When the ox is leanest he is best for work.
30. Five days of sowing, the three last of March and the two first of April.
31. One must have means to dress land.
32. While the harrow moves let the mill move.
33. As long as the harrow goes the thorn hurdle will go.
34. Heavy crops, wet harvest.

AMDDIFFYNIAD.

1. A gais nodded gofyned i'r cadarnaf.
2. Goreu amddiffynfa, digon pell.
3. Goreu nawdd, nawdd Duw.
4. Nid amddiffyn ond tarian.

AMMOD.

1. Ammod a dŷr ddefod.
2. Goreu ammod, cyfiawnder.
3. Trech ammod na chyfraith.
4. Trech ammod na gwir.

AMSER.

1. Amser a â heibio,
    Wrth chwareu ac wrth weithio.
2. Amser i fwyd, amser i olochwyd (addoliad.)

PROTECTION.

1. He who seeks protection let him ask the strongest.
2. The best place of defence is a sufficient distance.
3. The best protection is the protection of God.
4. The only defence is a shield.

AGREEMENT.

1. An agreement will break a custom.
2. The best agreement is justice.
3. An agreement is stronger than law.
4. A covenant is stronger than right.

TIME.

1. Time swiftly flies away,
    Whether we work or play.
2. Time for food, time for worship.

3. Nid hawdd attal amser.
4. Nid hawdd cuddio rhag amser.
5. Nid yspail ond yspail amser.
6. Pob peth yn ei amser.
7. Rhag pob clwyf eli amser.
8. Y naill flwyddyn a fydd fam i ddyn,
   A'r llall ei elldrewyn (mam-yn-nghyfraith.)

AMYNEDD.

1. A fyno ei fodd porthed amynedd.
2. Amynedd yw mam pob doethineb.
3. Cadarn pob amyneddus.
4. Cas athraw heb amynedd.
5. Eli i bob dolur yw amynedd.
6. Llawer clwyfus da 'i amynedd.
7. Nerth deddfol ei amynedd.
8. Nerth gwenynen ei hamynedd.
9. Nerth synwyrol ei amynedd.
10. Ni cholles mam amynedd.
11. Nid amynedd ond ystyr.

3. It is not easy to detain time.
4. It is not easy to hide from time.
5. There is no spoiling like that of time.
6. Everything in its time.
7. For every wound the ointment of time.
8. One year will be a man's mother,
  And the other his mother-in-law.

PATIENCE.

1. He who would have his will let him cultivate patience.
2. Patience is the mother of all wisdom.
3. The patient is strong.
4. Hateful is a teacher without patience.
5. It is well to look after patience.
6. Many a sick person of good patience.
7. The strength of the orderly is his patience.
8. The strength of the bee its patience.
9. The strength of the sensible is his patience.
10. A mother has not lost her patience.
11. There is no patience but reflection.

ANFFAWD.

1. A fo diried (anffodus) ar fôr, diried hefyd ar dir.
2. Anffawd a ddaw tan redeg, ac a â ymaith dan ymlusgo.
3. Anffawd a gyrch yn mhob rhith.
4. Anhapus pob trwch (anffortunus.)
5. Ceisiaw diried yn ei dyddyn.
6. Diried a gaiff ddraen yn ei uwd.
7. Edwyn anffawd ei pherchen.
8. Gwell anffawd o'i gael nag o'i ofni.
9. Gwell yn y crochan nag yn y tân.
10. Gwell y drwg a wyddis na'r drwg na wyddis.
11. Mawr yw toraeth yr aflwydd.
12. Ni bu drwg i un na fai da i arall.
13. Ni chwythodd na bai da i rywun.
14. Ni ellir damwain na fo da i rai.
15. Ni rygelir dryglam (anffawd.)
16. Nid anffodus a gaffo ddaioni yn y diwedd.
17. Nid argywedda (niweidio) melldith ond i'r hwn a'i haeddo.
18. Nid drwg a ddwg a fo'n dda.

MISFORTUNE.

1. Unlucky at sea, unlucky on land.
2. Misfortune comes running and walks away slowly.
3. Misfortune comes in every form.
4. Unhappy is every unfortunate person.
5. To seek for the unlucky in his dwelling.
6. The unlucky will get a thorn in his porridge.
7. Misfortune knows its possessor.
8. A misfortune is better than the fear of it.
9. Better in the saucepan than in the fire.
10. Better the evil we know than that which we know not.
11. Great is the store of the unfortunate.
12. It is not evil for one but that it is good for another.
13. It never blows but that it is good for someone.
14. An accident cannot happen that is not good for some.
15. A misfortune cannot be altogether concealed.
16. He is not unfortunate who receives good in the end.
17. A curse will do no harm but to him that deserves it.
18. That is not evil which produces good.

19. Nid llwyr anffawd ond o bechod.
20. Nid oes anffawd nas gellir rhyw ffawd o hono.
21. Trychni nid hawdd ei ochel.

ANGEU.

1. A ddwg angeu nid adfer.
2. A fo marw ni moch (buan) welir.
3. A fo marw ni ymogelir.
4. Addfed angeu i hên.
5. Angeu a ddaw yn ddiogel.
6. Angeu a ddyfrys (a frysia.)
7. Angeu a gyrch ac nid adfer.
8. Angeu garw, drud a'i heirch.
9. Angeu pob rhian (pennaethiad) diau y daw.
10. Buan ar farch, buan i'r arch.
11. Buan i'r wledd, buan i'r bedd.
12. Ceugant (sicr) yw angeu.
13. Diwyl (digywilydd) yw angeu,
    Diwylach a edau (a edy.)

19. There is no thorough misfortune but through sin.
20. There is no misfortune out of which some good fortune may not be got.
21. It is not easy to avoid disaster.

DEATH.

1. What death takes it will not restore.
2. He who is dead will not be seen soon.
3. He that dies will not be run away from.
4. To the aged death is ripe.
5. Death will certainly come.
6. Death will hasten.
7. Death takes and will not restore.
8. Bold is he that chooses a violent death.
9. The death of every chieftain is certain to come.
10. Quick on a horse, quick to the coffin.
11. Quick to the feast, quick to the grave.
12. Death is certain.
13. Death is shameless,
    More shameless he whom death leaves,

14. Gwell angeu na byw annoeth.
15. Gwell bedd na buchedd anghenawl.
16. Gwell bedd na bywyd gwydfawr.
17. Gwell golaith (trengu) na gofid.
18. Gwell marw na hir nychdod.
19. Gwell marw na mynych ddifrod.
20. Hanbid gwell y ci o farw y llall.
21. Hiraeth am farw ni weryd.
22. Mae yn dost ar a ddymunai farw ;
    Mae yn dostach ar a'i ofno.
23. Marw, na fyddo yn Nuw.
24. Ni âd y môr marwolus ynddo.
25. Ni ludd golud angeu.
26. Ni pheirch yr angeu na sidan na phorphor.
27. Ni wybydd un perchen cnawd beth fydd a'i dien (ei diwedd.)
28. Nid dir (sicr) ond angeu.
29. Nid edrych yr angeu pwy deccaf ei dalcen.
30. Nid gwell yn y bedd boneddig na thaiog.
31. Nid hysbys i neb p'le bydd ei dywarchen.
32. Nid nawdd eing llyfrder (llwfrdra) rhag llaith (angeu.)

14. Better death than foolish living.
15. Better the grave than a life of need.
16. Better the grave than a vicious life.
17. Better death than affliction.
18. Better death than long sickness.
19. Death is better than frequent devastation.
20. Let the dog be better for the death of the other.
21. Regret for the dead will not avail.
22. It is hard on him who wishes to die;
    It is harder on him who fears death.
23. Dead, he who is not in God.
24. The sea will not let the dead remain in it.
25. Wealth will not keep death away.
26. Death respects neither silk nor purple.
27. No one knows what his end will be.
28. Nothing is certain but death.
29. Death regards not the fairest face.
30. The gentleman is no better in the grave than the villain.
31. No one knows where his grave will be.
32. The escape of cowardice will not protect from death.

33. Ofner ef na ofno angeu.
34. Pan fo marw y sarph bydd marw ei cholyn.
35. Rhag angeu ni ddiangc neb.
36. Trwy byrth angeu y cawn olwg ar fyd sydd well.
37. Un gyflwr pawb yn angeu.
38. Yn angeu ni thyccia ffo.
39. Yn mhob rhith y daw angeu.

ANGHEN.

1. Anghen a bair i hen wrach deithio.
2. Anghen a bryn ac a werth.
3. Anghen a dyr ddeddf.
4. Anghen a ddysg hên i redeg.
5. Anghen a ragwelir ni ddaw fyth ar ddoeth.
6. Anghen yw mam pob celfyddyd.
7. Anghwbl (anmherffaith) pob eisieu.
8. Asgwrn yr hên yn yr anghen.
9. Bu well i'r gŵr a grwydrws nag a fu farw rhag newyn.
10. Clyd pob clawdd i gardotyn.

33. Let him be feared who fears not death.
34. When the serpent dies its sting dies also.
35. No one can flee from death.
36. Through the gates of death we shall view a better world.
37. All are of one condition in death.
38. Flight from death will not avail.
39. Death will come in every form.

NECESSITY.

1. Necessity will make an old woman trot.
2. Necessity will buy and sell.
3. Necessity will break the law.
4. Necessity will teach the old to run.
5. Need that is foreseen will not come upon the old.
6. Necessity is the mother of art.
7. Imperfect is every want.
8. The bone of the old in case of necessity.
9. Better he who wandered than he who died of hunger.
10. Every hedge is comfortable to the beggar.

11. Digllon pob newynog.
12. Goreu eisieu, eisieu cyfoeth.
13. Goreu newyn, newyn arian.
14. Gwell anghen na chywilydd.
15. Gwell anghenog ar fôr nag anghenog y mynydd.
16. Hoff gan anghenog ei goelio.
17. Ni cherir newynog.
18. Ni ddiylch anghen ei borthi.
19. Ni ddyddawr (ni ofala) newynog pa yso.
20. Ni wyddis eisieu y ffynon onid êl yn hesp.
21. Ni ŵyr yr hwch lawn pa wich y wâg.
22. Ni ŵyr llawn gwyn anghenog.
23. Nid edrych newyn y teccaf.
24. Nid eisieu ond eisieu deall.
25. Nid gwiw gwylder rhag eisieu.
26. Nid ysgar anghenawg âg anhychfryd (syrthni.)
27. Nid ysgar newyn â diogi.
28. Tra fo y borfa yn tyfu y bydd marw y march.
29. Trech angen na dewis.

11. Every hungry is angry.
12. The best want is the want of wealth.
13. The best need is the need of money.
14. Better ~~necessity~~ want than shame.
15. Better the needy at sea than the needy of the mountain.
16. The needy likes to be believed.
17. The hungry are not loved.
18. Necessity will not thank being maintained.
19. The hungry cares not what he eats.
20. The want of the spring is not felt until it is dry.
21. The full sow knows not the squeak of the empty one.
22. The full knows not the complaint of the needy.
23. Famine heeds not the fairest.
24. There is no need but the want of intellect.
25. Bashfulness is of no avail against want.
26. The needy will not be separated from a sluggish disposition.
27. Hunger will not part from idleness.
28. While the grass is growing the steed will die.
29. Necessity is stronger than choice.

ANGHOF.

1. Allan o olwg allan o feddwl.
2. Cas anghofio câr a chyfaill.
3. Dotiedig pob anghofus.
4. Gnawd i anghofus ddwy daith.
5. Y gwr yn ceisio ei gaseg a'i gaseg dano.

ANGHYMEDROLDEB.

1. Adrysedd drais annoeth.
2. Byr ddryganian a wna hir ofal.
3. Cas ddyn a wnelo yn un dydd fel na allo wneuthur dim dranoeth.
4. Gormod o ddim nid yw dda.
5. Nid da rhy o ddim.
6. Yn mhob gormod y mae traha.

FORGETFULNESS.

1. Out of sight out of mind.
2. Odious is he who forgets relative and friends.
3. Confused is every forgetful.
4. The forgetful are apt to have two journeys.
5. Seeking his mare and his mare under him.

INTEMPERANCE.

1. Over-excess is the oppression of the unwise.
2. A short season of intemperance will cost long anxiety.
3. Odious he that does so much one day that he can do nothing the next.
4. Too much of anything is not good.
5. Excess of anything is not good.
6. In every excess there is presumption.

ANGHYSONDEB.

1. Adneu cyhyryn gan gath.
2. Berwi y dwfr a'i fwrw allan.
3. Bwrw dwfr i Hafren.
4. Bwrw heli yn y mori.
5. Bwyta llymru â mynawyd.
6. Cadach sidan a phin draen
   A thwll yn mlaen yr esgid.
7. Cadw ci a chyfarth fy hun.
8. Cneua mewn brwyn.
9. Cosyn glân mewn cawsellt budr.
10. Cyfrwy i fuwch.
11. Cyfrwy i hwch.
12. Dall yn barnu ar liwiau.
13. Dangos llwybr i gyfarwydd.
14. Diangc rhag y mŵg a syrthio i'r tân.
15. Dwyn dw'r dros afon.
16. Ennill nodwydd ddur a cholli y trosol haiarn.
17. Ennill y gronyn a cholli dau cymaint.

INCONSISTENCY.

1. To pawn a piece of flesh with a cat.
2. To boil the water and pour it out.
3. To pour water into the Severn.
4. To throw brine into the sea.
5. To eat flummery with an awl.
6. A silk handkerchief with a pin of thorn,
    And a hole in the point of the shoe.
7. To keep a dog and bark myself.
8. To gather nuts among the rushes.
9. A clean cheese in a dirty cheese-vat.
10. A saddle for a cow.
11. A saddle for a sow.
12. The blind judging colours.
13. To show the path to one that knows it.
14. To rush from the smoke and fall into the fire.
15. To carry water over the river.
16. To gain a needle and lose the iron-bar.
17. To earn a grain and lose twice as much.

18. Genau mwyalch ac archiad blaidd.
19. Gofyn i ddall a ydyw yn doriad gwawr.
20. Goganu'r bwyd a'i fwytta.
21. Gwerthu cig hwch a phrynu cig moch.
22. Gwerthu mêl i brynu peth melus.
23. Gyru halen i'r heledd (pwll halen.)
24. Gwlana ar yr afr.
25. Gyru yr hwyaid i gyrchu y gwyddau o'r dwfr.
26. Iach yn ymofyn meddyg.
27. Iro blonegau.
28. Llafar oen a chalon blaidd.
29. Modrwy aur yn nhrwyn hwch.
30. Myned â gogyr i'r afon.
31. Myned trwy yr afon a phont ar bwys.
32. Nid hawdd blingo âg elestren.
33. Nid hawdd gwlana ar yr afr.
34. Nid hawdd tynu mêr o bôst.
35. Pen punt a llosgwrn dimai.
36. Rhoi y càr o flaen y march.
37. Rhoi y pwn trymaf ar y march gwanaf.

18. The mouth of a blackbird with the request of a wolf.
19. To ask the blind if it is daybreak.
20. Finding fault with the food and eating it.
21. To sell a sow and buy bacon.
22. To sell honey to buy a sweet thing.
23. Sending salt to the salt-pit.
24. Gathering wool upon the goat.
25. Sending the ducks to fetch the geese from the water.
26. The healthy seeking a doctor.
27. To grease a lump of lard.
28. The voice of a lamb with the heart of a wolf.
29. A gold ring in a sow's snout.
30. To go with a sieve to fetch water.
31. To go through the river with a bridge on the spot.
32. It is not easy to flay with a flag-leaf.
33. It is not easy to gather wool on the goat.
34. It is not easy to draw marrow from a post.
35. A pound head and halfpenny tail.
36. Putting the car before the horse.
37. Putting the heaviest load on the weakest horse.

38. Rhoi'r dorth a gofyn y dafell.
39. Sôn am Awst ddydd Calangauaf.
40. Sôn am Awst wyliau y Nadolig.
41. Swylo (cynnilo) ar y cilyn diweddaf.
42. Yr oen yn dysgu i'r ddafad bori.
43. Ysnoden aur â gŵn carth.

ANNIBYNIAETH.

1. Ceisied pawb ddwfr i'w long.
2. Iawn i bawb gadw ei hun.
3. Pawb drosto ei hun, Duw dros bawb.
4. Safed pob llestr ar ei gwaelod ei hun.
5. Safed pob un ar ei draed ei hun.

ANNUWIOLDEB.

1. A fo drwg unwaith a wyr pa fodd i fod yn ddrwg eilwaith.
2. A wnel ddrwg aröed y llall.
3. A wnel mawrddrwg a rydd mawrelw.

38. To give the loaf and ask for the slice.
39. To speak of August in winter.
40. To speak of August at Christmas.
41. To save when reduced to the last scrap.
42. The lamb teaching the sheep to graze.
43. A gold lace with a hempen gown.

INDEPENDENCE.

1. Let everyone seek water for his boat.
2. It is right that everyone should keep himself.
3. Everyone for himself, and God for all.
4. Let every boat stand on its own bottom.
5. Let everyone stand on his own feet.

WICKEDNESS.

1. He that is bad once knows how to be bad a second time.
2. He that commits evil let him expect it.
3. He that commits a great evil will swear a great oath.

4. A wreiddio mewn drygioni,
   Anhawdd fydd ei gynghori.
5. Cais nyth y drwg yn nghesail gair da.
6. Cas dyn a wnelo ddrwg ac ni bo edifar ganddo.
7. Ceir y drwg yn mhob man.
8. Crefydd a ladd y drwg, nid yw moes ond ei guddio.
9. Drwg un, drwg arall.
10. Drwg yw y drwg, a gwaeth yw y gwaethaf.
11. Drwg yw drwg yn mhob agwedd.
12. Drwg yw drwg yn mhob anian.
13. Drwg yw drwg yn mhob tafod.
14. Drwg yw y deg ewin.
15. Gair drwg anianol a lusg ddrwg yn ei ol.
16. Gnawd i Dduw gashau pechod.
17. Gochel y pechod cyntaf, canys y mae lleng yn dỳn wrth ei sawdl.
18. Goreu o'r drygau, y lleiaf.
19. Gormod yw bychod (ychydig) o bechodau.
20. Gwaethaf anaf, anfoes.
21. Gwisgi pob troed at y drwg.
22. Hawdd cael drwg ac anhawdd myned oddiwrtho.

4. It is difficult to advise him who is rooted in wickedness.

5. Seek the nest of evil in the bosom of a good word.
6. Odious is he who does evil and repents not.
7. Evil is met with everywhere.
8. Religion kills evil, morality only hides it.
9. Evil one, evil another.
10. Bad is bad, and worse is the worst.
11. Evil is evil in every form.
12. Evil is evil in every nature.
13. Evil is evil in every tongue.
14. The ten fingers are evil.
15. An evil sensual word drags evil after it.
16. It is natural for God to hate sin.
17. Avoid the first sin, for a legion follows at its heel.

18. The best evils are the smallest.
19. A few sins are too many.
20. The worst blemish is immorality.
21. Every foot is brisk towards evil.
22. It is easy to receive evil and difficult to avoid it.

23. Ni aned ni wyddiad (ni ŵyr) bechod.
24. Ni bu ddrwg erioed heb ferch yn rhywben.
25. Ni chafodd ddrwg mae yn ei aros.
26. Ni ludd doethineb pechod.
27. Nid drwg ond a dybio ei hun yn dda.
28. Nid drwg ond a geffir drwg o hono.
29. Nid drwg ond drwg yn ymgêl.
30. Nid ellir drwg heb ryw dda o hono.
31. Nid gwrth ar y drwg ond Duw.
32. Nid hawdd diangc o ddrwg.
33. Nid hawdd galw y drwg yn ol.
34. Nid pechod ond temtasiwn.
35. Nid syrthni ond pechod.
36. Nid ymgêl drwg lle y bo.
37. O ddau ddrwg goreu y lleiaf.
38. Pe gwelai annuwioldeb ei ddiwedd byddai farw gan ddychryn.
39. Trymaf baich, baich o bechod.
40. Un pechod a lusg gant ar ei ol.
41. Ymrith y drwg ar lun daioni.
42. Yn mhob drwg y mae a'i cysb.
43. Yn mhob drygioni y mae pechod.
44. Yn mhob pechod y mae ffoledd.

23. He is not born who knows not sin.
24. There never was evil without a female at some end.
25. He who has not met evil awaits it.
26. Wisdom will not prevent sin.
27. There is none evil but he who thinks himself evil.
28. Nothing is evil but that from which evil is obtained.
29. There is no evil but evil in concealment.
30. There is no evil without some good in it.
31. There is no opposition to evil but God.
32. It is not easy to flee from evil.
33. It is not easy to call evil back.
34. There is no sin but temptation.
35. The essence of torpitude is sin.
36. Evil will not be concealed.
37. Of two evils the least is the best.
38. If wickedness saw its end it would die of fright.

39. The heaviest load is the load of sin.
40. One sin draws a hundred after it.
41. Evil will shew itself in the form of good.
42. In all evil there is that which will punish.
43. In all evil there is sin.
44. In all sin there is folly.

ANONESTRWYDD.

1. A ddygo yr ŵy a ddwg a fo mwy.
2. A ddygo yr ŵy a ddwg yr iar.
3. Arwaesaf i leidr ei fynag (ei fynegiad.)
4. Cyntaf yn lleidr, cyntaf yn frenin.
5. Gnawd i leidr ddod i'r ddalfa.
6. Gnawd i leidr ei hir ymlid.
7. Gnawd lledrad yn ddiymgel.
8. Hir ladrad i grôg.
9. Hoff yw gan leidr dywyllwch.
10. Llofrudd pob lleidr.
11. March-leidr a grôg y cor-leidr.
12. Melys yw cig lladrad.
13. Neb a dyno nyth y dryw,
    Ni cheiff iechyd yn ei fyw.
14. Nid hawdd lladrata oddiar leidr.

DISHONESTY.

1. He who steals an egg will steal what is greater.
2. He who steals the egg will steal the hen.
3. A warrant for a thief is his own declaration.
4. First a thief, first a king.
5. It is natural for a thief to be caught.
6. A thief is generally long pursued.
7. Theft will be made manifest.
8. Long theft to the gallows.
9. The thief likes darkness.
10. Every thief is a murderer.
11. The great thief will hang the petty thief.
12. Sweet is stolen meat.
13. He who disturbs the wren's nest,
    With health he will ne'er be bles't.
14. It is not easy to rob a thief.

ANRHYDEDD.

1. A gaffo air da unwaith ef a chwenych ei gadw a'i gynnal.
2. Ceinmygir (anrhydeddir) pob newydd.
3. Deuparth anrhydedd, moes.
4. Deuparth urddas, enw da.
5. Dyn a urdd y lle, ac nid y lle y dyn.
6. Enw heb senw.
7. Na chais urddas o falchder.
8. Nid anrhydedd ond byw mewn hedd.
9. Nid anrhydedd ond gwybodaeth.
10. Nid prophwyd neb yn ei wlad ei hun.
11. Nid syberwyd heb haelioni.
12. Nid treftad anrhydedd arglwydd.
13. Nid urddas ond gwybodaeth.
14. Odid urddas o drais.
15. Pawb a chwennych anrhydedd.
16. Yn mhob anrhydedd y mae urddas.

HONOUR.

1. He who once gets a good name desires to keep and sustain it.
2. Everything new is honoured.
3. Two parts of honour is morality.
4. Two parts of dignity is a good name.
5. Man honours the station, not the station the man.
6. A name without dignity.
7. Seek not honour from pride.
8. There is no honour but to live in peace.
9. There is no honour but knowledge.
10. No one is a prophet in his own country.
11. There is no honour without liberality.
12. The honour of a lord is not an inheritance.
13. There is no dignity without knowledge.
14. Seldom comes honour from oppression.
15. All men covet honour.
16. In every honour there is respect.

ANUDONIAETH.

1. Aflan genau anudonawl.
2. Cas a dyngo lŵ anudon hyd nes credo neb ef.

3. Cas geudyst yn nghynghaws.
4. Na chais nef o'th anudon.
5. Na fid esgud dy law ar lŵ anudon.
6. Nid anudon ymchwelid ar y da.

ANWIREDD.

1. A fo'n iawn ni fyn anwir.
2. Arianoedd, neu aur ennyd,
    A wna'r gau yn wir i gyd.
3. Beth wedi celwydd? cernawd.
4. Bost a chelwydd nid deubeth ydynt.
5. Brawd yw celwyddog i leidr.
6. Celwydd o ben un, gwir o bennau pawb.
7. Cas dyn ni chredo neb, na neb yntau.

8. Gnawd i gelwyddog gochi.

PERJURY.

1. Polluted are the perjured lips.
2. Odious is he who commits perjury until no one believes him.
3. Odious is a false witness in an action.
4. Seek not heaven from thy false swearing.
5. Be not swift to commit perjury.
6. It is no perjury to break a resolution to produce good.

FALSEHOOD.

1. He that is just will not bear with falsehood.
2. A large sum of silver or gold,
   Will make all falsehood true.
3. What after falsehood? a blow.
4. Boast and falsehood are not two things.
5. The liar and thief are brothers.
6. Falsehood from the one, truth from the many.
7. Hateful is he who believes no one, and whom no one believes.
8. It is natural for a liar to blush.

9. Goreu celwydd, celwydd amlwg.
10. Goreu cerddedydd, gau (anwiredd.)
11. Nid anhylwydd ond y celwydd.
12. Nid celwyddwr ond bostiwr.
13. Nid hawdd cadarnhau celwydd.
14. Nid oes air celwydd heb ynddo dwyll a brâd.
15. Nid oes anwiredd heb waradwydd ac alaeth.
16. Rhaid côf da i ddywedyd celwydd.
17. Tywyll fydd gau, golau gwir.
18. Ymborth anwiredd yw aur ac arian.

ANWYBODAETH.

1. Ammeu pob anwybod.
2. Anwybodus a ddengys yn fuan a wyr, fel plentyn yn dangos tegan.
3. Dallaf o'r dall, dyn diddeall.
4. Dïwybod pob diymgais.
5. Goreu y celid peth nis gwypid.
6. Ni ŵyr neb lai na'n hwn a ŵyr y cyfan.
7. Nid annysgedig a ŵyr ddysgu da i arall.

9. The best falsehood is an evident falsehood.
10. The best traveller is falsehood.
11. There is nothing so unprosperous as falsehood.
12. There is no liar like the boaster.
13. It is not easy to confirm falsehood.
14. There is no falsehood withot deceit and treachery in it.
15. There is no falsehood without reproach and sorrow.
16. It requires a good memory to tell lies.
17. Falsehood shall be dark and truth illumined.
18. The food of falsehood is gold and silver.

IGNORANCE.

1. Every ignorance is doubtful.
2. The ignorant soon shews what he knows, as a child shews its toy.
3. The blindest of the blind is an ignorant man.
4. The unambitious is ignorant.
5. It is best to conceal that which is not known.
6. No one knows less than he who knows all.
7. He is not ignorant who knows how to teach good to another.

8. Nid anwybodus ond a dybio ei fod yn gwybod y cyfan.
9. Nid hawdd cydfod â diwybod.
10. Nid hawdd darwedd anwybodus.
11. Nid hawdd tynu mêr o bost.

ARFER.

1. Ail natur yw greddf arferiad.
2. Anmraint pob tòr defod.
3. Arfer a ddaw haner y ffordd i gyfarfod â phob ymgais.
4. Arfer a wna meistri.
5. Arfer a wna yn hawdd y pethau mwyaf anhawdd.
6. Arfer anarfer yw yr arfer waethaf yn y byd.
7. Arfer sydd drech na deddf.
8. Arfer yw haner y gwaith.
9. Arfer yw mam meistrolaeth.
10. Arfer a ddwg pob peth dan ei wedd.
11. Deuparth tref ei harferau.
12. Goreu arfer, doethineb.
13. Goreu defod, daioni.

8. There is none ignorant but he who thinks he knows all.
9. It is not easy to co-exist with the ignorant.
10. It is not easy to direct the ignorant.
11. It is not easy to draw marrow from a post.

PRACTICE.

1. Practice is second nature.
2. Every violation of custom is a breach of privilege.
3. Practice comes half way to meet every effort.
4. Use makes masters.
5. Use makes the most difficult things easy.
6. To be in the habit of no habit is the worse habit in the world.
7. Custom is mightier than law.
8. Practice is half the work.
9. Practice is the mother of mastership.
10. Custom brings everything under its yoke.
11. Two-thirds of a town are its customs.
12. The best custom is wisdom.
13. The best custom is rectitude.

14. Goreu defod, ymwellhau.
15. Gwell nag athraw yw arfer.
16. Hên arfer hon a orfydd.
17. Llawaidd (celfydd) pob cynhefin.
18. Meistr pob gwaith yw ymarfer.
19. Moes pob tud yn ei dud.
20. Pob gwlad yn ei harfer.
21. Trech arfer nag arfaeth.
22. Ys dir y llwydd llaw gyfarwydd.

ARIAN.

1. Arian a bryn ac a werth.
2. Ceir pob peth am arian.
3. Da i wr ydyw arian.
4. Diwedd y gân yw y geiniog.
5. Drwg y geiniog a feflo ei pherchenog.
6. Goreu cydymaith, ceiniog.
7. Goreu parodrwydd, arian.
8. Goreu cyfaill, bathodyn.

14. The best habit is to improve one's self.
15. Practice is better than a teacher.
16. An old custom will prevail.
17. Every practised hand is handy.
18. Practice is the master of every work.
19. The custom of every place in its place.
20. Every country agreeable to its custom.
21. Habit is stronger than resolution.
22. The practised hand is sure to prosper.

MONEY.

1. Money will buy and sell.
2. Everything can be obtained for money.
3. Money is good for man.
4. The end of the song is money.
5. Bad the penny that disgraces its possessor.
6. The best companion is a penny.
7. The best readiness is money.
8. The best friend is a piece of silver,

9. Gwell ceiniog na brawd.
10. Llyswen mewn dwfr yw arian.
11. Nid trwyddedawg ond dinair.
12. Pob un a gâr lle ceir arian.

BAI.

1. A ddadla dros ei fai a wna ddau ddiawl o un cythraul.

2. Aml bai lle nis cerir.
3. Ar bennaeth bai fydd amlwg.
4. Câs a fëio ac yntau yn fëius.
5. Câs bëio ar waith Duw.
6. Câs bëio ar y bwyd a'i fwytta.
7. Câs a ogano arall am y beiau fo arno ef ei hun.

8. Câs ddyn a ŵyr ei fai ac nas diwygia.
9. Ef a gair gwall ar y callaf.
10. Heb ei fai, heb ei eni.
11. Ni bydd neb llyfn heb ei anaf.
12. Na feia ar neb am y bai a fo arnat dy hun.
13. Ni fyn neb gydnabod ei fai.

9. Better a penny than a brother.
10. Money is like an eel in the hand.
11. There is no free traveller like a penny.
12. All love where there is money.

FAULT.

1. He that pleads for his fault makes two devils out of one fiend.
2. Many the faults where there is no love.
3. On a chief a fault is conspicuous.
4. Odious is he who blames when he is himself at fault.
5. Odious is he who blames God's work.
6. Odious is he who finds fault with the food and eats it.
7. Hateful is he who blames another for the faults he has himself.
8. Hateful is he who knows his fault and reforms not.
9. The wisest has his fault.
10. He who is faultless is not born.
11. There is nothing smooth without its blemish.
12. Blame no one for the fault which is in thyself.
13. No one likes to own his fault.

14. Ni wyl diriaid arno fai.
15. Nid oes neb heb ei fai.
16. O chwenychi droi dyn oddiwrth ei fai rho iddo air da.
17. Tew y beiau lle teneu y cariad.

BALCHDER.

1. A ddringo yn rhy uchel fe dyr y brigyn dano.
2. Balch Cymro ar ei wlad.
3. Balch yw hwyaid ar y gwlaw.
4. Balchder a bair cynhen
5. Balchder a'i gydymaith
    A gafas gwymp ar unwaith.
6. Balchder heb droed.
7. Can falched o'i gŵd ag yntau o'i sach.
8. Enwog mychiad o'i foch.
9. Ffol pob balch.
10. Gnawd i uchelfryd gwympo.
11. Hawdd ffromi balch.
12. Lle blaena balchder y canlyna cywilydd,

14. The mischievous sees no fault in himself.
15. There is no one without his fault.
16. If you wish to turn a man from his fault give him a good word.
17. Faults are thick where love is thin.

PRIDE.

1. He who climbs too high the sprig will break under him.
2. The Welshman is proud of his country.
3. Proud are ducks in the rain.
4. Pride leads to contention.
5. Pride and its companion
   Had a fall together.
6. Pride without a foot.
7. As proud of his bag as he of his sack.
8. A swineherd is proud of his swine.
9. Every proud person is foolish.
10. The lofty are apt to fall.
11. It is easy to irritate the haughty.
12. Where pride leads, shame follows.

13. Meddw pob balch ar waddawd ei annoethineb.
14. Na chais urddas o falchder.
15. Nid balch ond alarch.
16. Nid gwallgof ond balchder.
17. Nid oes falchder heb iddo ostyngiad.
18. Pe gwelai falch ei galon fe gollai ei holl synwyrau gan arswyd.
19. Ufudd-dod i gyfoeth a balchder i dylodi.

BARN.

1. Ar ddiwedd y mae barnu.
2. Barn arnat dy hun yn gyfiawn a Duw a'th fechnïa.
3. Câs barn heb ddangosau.
4. Haws barnu na saethu saeth.
5. Moch (buan) barn pob ehud.
6. Ni bydd brawd (barn) heb ei hadfrawd.
7. Ni eill barnu ni wrandawo.
8. Nid a farn yn gyfiawn ond Duw.
9. Nid barn ond barn Duw.
10. Rhydd i bawb ei farn.

13. Every proud one is intoxicated with the dregs of his ignorance.
14. Do not seek dignity from pride.
15. There is none so proud as the swan.
16. There is no madness but pride.
17. There is no pride without humiliation.
18. If the proud could see his heart he would be frightened out of his senses.
19. Humility to wealth and pride to poverty.

JUDGMENT.

1. One should judge at the conclusion.
2. Pass sentence on thyself equitably and God will become thy surety.
3. Odious is judgment without demonstration.
4. It is easier to judge than to shoot.
5. Hasty is the judgment of every fool.
6. There will be no judgment without its contradiction.
7. He cannot judge who will not listen.
8. None judge rightly but God.
9. There is no judgment but the judgment of God.
10. Judgment is free to all.

BENTHYG.

1. Câs a echwyno cymaint ag na bo ganddo a'i talo.
2. Câs a ddycco yn echwyn mwy nag allo dalu byth.
3. Dod fenthyg i noeth
    Nis cei dranoeth.
4. Echwyn yw nag.
5. Gwell benthyg nac eisiau.
6. Llwm ŷch llog.
7. Na ddyro echwyn heb edrych i bwy.
8. Tw ! farch benthyg.
9. Y neb fo a march ganddo a geiff farch yn menthyg.

BODDLONRWYDD.

1. Abl yw soeg i foch.
2. Addas i bawb a'i boddlono.
3. Cyfoethog pob boddlon.
4. Digon i bawb a gaffo.
5. Digon pob boddlondeb.

BORROWING.

1. Odious is he who borrows so much as not to have anything to repay with.
2. Odious is he who borrows more than he can ever pay.
3. Lend to the naked,
    You will not get it on the morrow.
4. A denial is what is upon trust.
5. Better to borrow than want.
6. Bare is the hired ox.
7. Lend not without considering to whom.
8. Gee on! hired horse.
9. He who has a horse can borrow one.

CONTENTMENT.

1. Draff is sufficient for pigs.
2. Proper to everyone what satisfies him.
3. The contented are rich.
4. Sufficient to everyone is what he receives.
5. Sufficient is every contentment.

6. Digon yw digon o fêl.
7. Gwell bodd pawb na'i anfodd.
8. Llawer tlawd a wêl ei ddigon.
9. Na chais amgen nag a fo Duw yn ddanfon,
   A phynag y bo bydd di foddlon.
10. Ni fu erioed ddigon na fyddai beth yn ol.
11. Ni waeth digon na gormod.
12. Nid digonedd ond boddlonedd.
13. Nid gwell gormod na rhy fychan.
14. Nid gwell gormod na digon.
15. Nid hawdd boddloni pawb.

BRYS.

1. Gnawd edifeirwch o frys.
2. Gnawd gwedi rhedeg attregwch (oediad.)
3. Mwyaf y brys, mwyaf y rhwystr.
4. Rhuthyr enderig o'r allt.
5. Yr hai (brys) a laddodd yr hwch.

6. Sufficient is sufficient honey.
7. The goodwill of everyone is better than his displeasure.
8. Many a poor man is satisfied.
9. Seek no more than God sends,
   And whatever it is be satisfied.
10. There never was plenty but that there was some to spare.
11. Enough is as good as too much.
12. There is no sufficiency but contentment.
13. Excess is no better than too little.
14. Too much is no better than enough.
15. It is not easy to please everyone.

HAST E.

1. Repentance is apt to follow haste.
2. A stoppage is usual after a run.
3. The more the haste the greater the hinderance.
4. The run of the steer from the hill.
5. The hurry has killed the sow.

BYDDARDOD.

1. Hir y bydd y mud yn mhorth y byddar.
2. Ni chenir cloch i fyddar.
3. Ni thâl husting (sisial) â byddar.
4. Tyn y cŵyr o'th glustiau.

BYGYTHIAD.

1. Câs a fygythio pawb ac ni bo ar neb ei ofn.
2. Gwell bygwth na tharo.
3. Gwell ci a gyfartho na chi a gnotho.
4. Nag ymddiried i'r neb a'th fygythio.
5. Ni ladd gogyfaddaw (bygwth.)
6. Y cyfiawn a wna ei swydd er bygythion.

BYWYD.

1. A fwrw ymaith ei fywyd yn ddiachos marw dros y diawl y mae.
2. A hauo dyn hyd einioes
    A feda ef wedi oes.

DEAFNESS.

1. Long will the dumb be at the gate of the deaf.
2. A bell is not rung for the deaf.
3. It is useless to whisper to the deaf.
4. Take the wax out of your ear.

THREATS.

1. Odious is he who threatens everyone and whom no one fears.
2. Better threaten than strike.
3. Better a dog that barks than one that devours.
4. Trust not the one that threatens.
5. Threats will not kill.
6. The just will do his duty in spite of threats.

LIFE.

1. He who without a cause throws away his life dies for the devil.
2. What man sows during his lifetime,
   He will reap afterwards.

3. Anhawdd gado'r bywyd.
4. Bywyd bod yn Nuw.
5. Duw a rân hyd yr einioes.
6. Gwell byw na marw.
7. Hoedl dyn nid gelyn a'i rhân.
8. Ni chain ymddiried i hir einioes.
9. Ni cheffir hoedl hir er ymgeledd.
10. Nid bywyd heb ryddid.
11. Nid bywyd ond gair Duw.

CANMOLIAETH.

1. A fedro ganmol, canmoled y penaf.
2. Balch pob moledig.
3. Canmawl doeth trach ei gefn, a merch o flaen ei gwyneb.
4. Canmawl dy fro a thrig yno.
5. Canmoled pawb y bont a'i dycco drosodd.
6. Canmoled pawb y rhyd mal y caffo.
7. Gnawd o'i ganmol canmoladwy.
8. Moliant gwedi marw.
9. Molir pawb wrth ei waith.
10. Ni raid i Arthur wrth ffyn baglau.

3. It is difficult to leave life.
4. To be in God is life.
5. God divides the duration of life.
6. Better to live than die.
7. An enemy has not the disposal of man's life.
8. It will not do to trust to long life.
9. Long life is not obtained through care.
10. There is no life without freedom.
11. There is no life but the word of God.

PRAISE.

1. He who can praise let him praise the greatest.
2. The commended is proud.
3. Praise the wise behind his back and a female to her face.
4. Praise thy country and dwell there.
5. Let all praise the bridge that carries them over.
6. Let all praise the ford as they find it.
7. He who is praised is apt to become praiseworthy.
8. Praise after death.
9. All are praised according to their work.
10. Arthur needs no crutches.

CAREDIGRWYDD.

1. Da cofio cymwynas.
2. Goreu ar bob gwynfyd ymgymwynasu.
3. Goreu caredigrwydd, ceryddu pechod.
4. Nid caredig ond gwâr.

CARIAD.

1. A garer neu gaseir a welir o bell.
2. A garo ei fam cared ei elltrewyn.
3. A garo yr iau (yr ieuengaf) cared ei chwarëuon.
4. A'm caro i cared fy nghi.
5. Amlwg câs a chariad.
6. Câr pawb nod dy elyn.
7. Câr y dyn da, ac nag anghar y dyn drwg.
8. Cariad a orchfyga bobpeth.
9. Cariad yw mam pob dwyfoldeb.
10. Câs brodyr heb gariad.
11. Chwerddid bryd wrth a garer.
12. Deuparth daioni, cariad.

KINDNESS.

1. It is well to remember a good turn.
2. The best of every happiness is mutual kindness.
3. The best kindness is to rebuke sin.
4. There are none kind but the gentle.

LOVE.

1. He who is loved or hated is seen afar off.
2. He who loves his mother let him love his stepmother.
3. He who loves the younger let him love his plays.
4. He who loves me let him love my dog.
5. Hatred and love are conspicuous.
6. Love everybody, even an enemy.
7. Love the good man and do not hate the bad man.
8. Love will conquer everything.
9. Love is the mother of all godliness.
10. Hateful are brothers without love.
11. Be gladdened the mind with such as is loving.
12. Two parts of goodness is love.

13. Duw a gâr a garo ei hunan.
14. Gwae a gâr ac ni garer.
15. Gwell cariad y ci na'i gâs.
16. Hawdd cymmod lle bo cariad.
17. Hawdd cyneu tân yn hen aelwyd.
18. Hawdd eiriol lle y carer.
19. Heb serch, heb synwyr.
20. Hygar pawb wrth a garo.
21. Na chais gariad o falchedd.
22. Namyn cariad nid oes Duw.
23. Namyn cariad nid oes gwynfyd.
24. Namyn cariad nid oes nef.
25. Namyn Duw nid oes gariad.
26. Ni châr morwyn mab o'i thrêf.
27. Ni charo ei fam cared ei lysfam.
28. Ni cherir yn llwyr oni ddelo'r ŵyr.
29. Ni fyn cariad ei wadu
      Na'i ddangos i luaws lu.
30. Nid caredig ond cariadus.
31. Nid cariad heb dangnef.
32. Nid cariad heb gyfiawnder.
33. Nid cariad heb haelioni.
34. Nid cariad ond cyfiawnder.
35. Nid cariad ond Duw.
36. Nid oes na farw namyn serch.
37. Nid rhaid tafod i draethu serch.
38. Nid serchog ond ëos.
39. Nid ymgêl cariad lle bo.
40. Nid ynfydrwydd ond tra-serch.
41. Oer yw y cariad a ddiffydd ar un chwa o wynt.
42. Pawb a gâr ei gywala.

13. God loves him who loves himself.
14. Woe to him who loves and is not loved.
15. Better a dog's love than his hatred.
16. It is easy to reconcile where there is love.
17. It is easy to kindle fire on an old hearth.
18. It is easy to intercede where there is love.
19. Without love, without sense.
20. Everyone is pleasing to the one he loves.
21. Seek not love from pride.
22. Besides love there is no God.
23. Except love there is no happiness.
24. Besides love there is no heaven.
25. Besides God there is no love.
26. A damsel loves not a youth from her own hamlet.
27. He that loves not his mother let him love his mother-in-law.
28. There will be no loving completely until the grandchild comes.
29. Love neither cares to be denied,
    Nor shewn to numbers far and wide.
30. None are loved but the loving.
31. There is no love without peace.
32. There is no love without justice.
33. There is no love without liberality.
34. There is no love but justice.
35. There is no love but God.
36. There is nothing that dies not but love.
37. A tongue is not necessary for declaring love.
38. There is nothing so loving as the nightingale.
39. Love will not be concealed.
40. There is no foolishness like excess of love.
41. Cold is the love that is put out by one blast of wind.
42. Everyone loves his fellow.

43. Pe gwelai serch ei wendid ef a drengai gan ofn.
44. Trech serch na chawr.
45. Yn mhob maddeu y mae cariad.

CARTREF.

1. Ar ol rhodio pob lle hawddfyd i gartref.
2. Cais annoeth yn mhob man eithr yn nghartref.
3. Cais ddedwydd yn ei gartref.
4. Cais ddoeth yn ei dyddyn.
5. Castell pawb, ei dŷ.
6. Gwedi treiglo pob tref,
    Teg edrych tuag adref.
7. Gwell bwth yn gartref,
    Na llys yn alldref.
8. Gwell tu fewn i fwthyn na thu allan i gastell.
9. Ni charo ei dref,
    Ni cheiff y nef.
10. Ni charo ei gartref yn y byd hwn, ni cheiff gartref yn y byd a ddaw.
11. Nid tref ond nef.
12. Symudaw addef rhag drwg.
13. Y dyn a wertho ei dŷ yn mha wlad y ceiff letty?

43. If love could see its weakness it would die of fright.
44. Love is stronger than a giant.
45. In every pardon there is love.

HOME.

1. After travelling everywhere pleasant is home.
2. Seek the foolish everywhere but at home.
3. Seek the happy at home.
4. Seek the wise in his cottage.
5. Everyone's house is his castle.
6. When far away in distant lands we roam,
    How pleasant 'tis to turn our footsteps home.
7. Better a cottage for a home than a palace to visit as a stranger.
8. Better inside a cottage than outside a castle.
9. He who loves not his home will not see heaven.
10. He who loves not his home in this world will not have a home in the world to come.
11. There is no home but heaven.
12 To remove a dwelling from evil.
13. He who sells his house in what country will he obtain lodging?

CASINEB.

1. Amlwg câs a chariad.
2. Bydd anfwyn wrth anfwyn o'th anfodd.
3. Câs a gasäo pawb a phawb yntau.

4. Câs gan ddrwg ddrwg yn arall.
5. Câs gan y gath y ci a'i bratho.
6. Câs myharen mieri.
7. Gnawd rhygas wedi rhyserch.
8. Na chwsg awr â châs gwiriawn.
9. Namyn câs nid oes gythraul.
10. Namyn câs nid oes uffern.
11. Ni chydfydd câs â gwirionedd.
12. Nid hir y celir cilwg.
13. Po fwyaf y câs mwyaf y cywilydd.
14. Rhygas rhywelir.
15. Yn mhob câs y mae gelyniaeth.

CELLWAIR.

1. Câs a gellwair â phawb ac ni oddef gellwair gan neb.
2. Câs cellwair â hên ddyn.
3. Euog a dry y cellwair yn wir.
4. Na chais gellwair â'th gâs.

HATRED.

1. Hatred and love are conspicuous.
2. Be unkind to the unkindly against thy will.
3. Odious is he who hates everyone and who is hated by everyone.
4. Evil hates evil in another.
5. The cat hates the dog that bites her.
6. The rams dislike the briars.
7. Extreme hatred is usual after extreme fondness.
8. Sleep not an hour with foolish enmity.
9. Except hatred there is no devil.
10. Except hatred there is no hell.
11. Hatred and truth cannot live together.
12. A grudge will not be long concealed.
13. The greater the hatred the greater the shame.
14. The extremely hated will be seen too soon.
15. In every hatred there is hostility.

JOKES.

1. Odious is he who jokes with everyone and will not allow anyone to joke with him.
2. Odious are they who joke with an old man.
3. The guilty will turn jesting to truth.
4. Do not joke with an enemy.

CENFIGEN.

1. A fyno ddrwg i'w gymydog iddo ei hun y daw.
2. Athrodwaith o genfigen.
3. Cenfigen a ladd ei pherchen.
4. Da gan y naill gi grogi y llall.
5. Ffolaf dyn, y cenfigenllyd.
6. Nid hawdd gostegu cenfigen.
7. Nid hawdd rhadloni cenfigen.
8. Nid pwyllig y dyn a ddalia genfigen.
9. Odid da diwarafun.

CERDDORIAETH.

1. A gano yn ei wely a grïa cyn cysgu.
2. Brodyr pob cerddorion.
3. Deuparth cerdd, ei gwrandaw.
4. Gnawd i fuddugol ganu.
5. Gwell cerdd o'i breiniaw.
6. Gwell canu hwyr na chanu boreu.
7. Haws cân hwyr na chân boreu.
8. Na thebyg mai doeth y ceir pob cerddor.

ENVY.

1. He who wishes his neighbour evil it will come to himself.
2. Defamation from mere malice.
3. Envy will kill its possessor.
4. One dog likes to hang another.
5. The most foolish of men is the envious.
6. It is not easy to silence malice.
7. It is not easy to render malice generous.
8. He who harbours envy is not prudent.
9. Seldom is there a benefit unenvied.

MUSIC.

1. He who sings in bed will cry before he sleeps.
2. All musicians are brothers.
3. Two parts of a song, the hearing of it.
4. The victorious are apt to sing.
5. A song is the better for being privileged.
6. Better late singing than early singing.
7. Easier is the evening song than the morning song.
8. Do not expect to find every musician wise.

9. Nid â bwyall y mae canu crwth.
10. Nid pob dyn cryf a fedr ganu telyn.

CERYDD.

1. A eiriach (arbed) ei wialen a ddifwyna ei fachgen.
2. Cerydd dy hun, na cherydd arall.
3. Gwae y tŷ lle nas clywir llais cerydd
4. Gwaeth na chledd cerydd doethion.
5. Nis ceryddo Duw nis ceryddaf.

COF.

1. Côf a lithra, llythyr a geidw.
2. Côf gan bawb a gâr.
3. Côf gan octid (ieuenctyd) ys dir.
4. Da yw côf mab.
5. Goreu côf, côf llyfr.
6. Ni chofia y chwegr pan fu waudd.
7. O gadw dy gôf y cedwi ddoethineb.

9. It is not with an axe that the violin is played.
10. It is not every strong man that can play the harp.

REBUKE.

1. He who spares his rod spoils his boy.
2. Rebuke thyself, not others.
3. Woe to the house where the voice of reproof is not heard.
4. The rebuke of the wise is worse than a sword.
5. Whom God rebukes not, I rebuke not.

MEMORY.

1. Memory will slip, a letter will keep.
2. Everyone thinks of the one he loves.
3. Memory with youth is certain.
4. The memory of a child is good.
5. The best record is that of a book.
6. The mother-in-law does not remember being daughter-in-law.
7. Keep your memory and you will keep wisdom.

CÔSP.

1. A garo Duw a gospa.
2. A hoffo ei rosb hoffed a'i cosp.

3. Cosp ar ben iar.
4. Cospi y maer yn mhen y dref.
5. Cospi yr arth yn ngwydd y llew.
6. Gwell dyn drwg o'i gospi.
7. Nid â cosp ar ynfyd.
8. Nid caled ond cosp.
9. Nid cosp ond dioddef o anfodd.

CREDINIAETH.

1. Coelia'n llai'r glust na'r golwg.
2. Cred air o bob deg a glywi a thi a gei rywfaint bach o wir.
3. Dylid coelio pob peth a choelio dim.
4. Goreu mawl, fy nghredu.
5. Gwae a gredo i bob chwedl a glywo.
6. Na chred byth ferch dy chwegrwn (tad-yn-nghyfraith.)
7. Na ro goel i newyddion oni bo'nt yn hên.
8. Ni choelir y moel oni welir ei ymenydd.

PUNISHMENT.

1. Whom God loves he chastizes.
2. He who loves his whim let him love the one that corrects it.
3. Chastisement on the hen's head.
4. Punishing the mayor at the head of the town.
5. To punish the bear in the presence of the lion.
6. A bad man is better for being punished.
7. Punishment does not move the fool.
8. There is nothing severe but punishment.
9. There is no punishment but suffering against one's will.

CREDULITY.

1. Believe the ear less than the eye.
2. Believe one word of every ten you hear and you will will get some truth.
3. One should believe everything and believe nothing.
4. My best praise is to be believed.
5. Woe to him who believes every story he hears.
6. Never believe your father-in-law's daughter.
7. Do not believe news until they are old.
8. The bald will not be believed unless his brains are seen.

9. Ni chred eiddig er a dynger.
10. Nid cred heb dystiolaeth.
11. Nid cred ond gwir.

CREULONDEB.

1. Dyrnawd gwas hir ei gâs.
2. Dywal dir fydd ei olaith.
3. Gnawd i greulon hir gâs.
4. Nid creulawn ond llew.
5. Nid ffyrnig ond ci.

CWSG.

1. Byr ei hûn, hir ei hoedl.
2. Da boreuwawr godi.
3. Ef a gwsg galarus, ac ni chwsg gofalus.
4. Hawdd cysgu mewn croen cyfa.
5. I gysgu gyda thrawd yr ŷch,
    A chodi gyda'r uchedydd.
6. Ni cheir da o hir gysgu.
7. Ni chwsg gwag fol.

9. Believe not the jealous even though he swears.
10. There is no belief without evidence.
11. There is no belief but truth.

CRUELTY.

1. A blow to a servant is long remembered.
2. The death of the fierce is certain.
3. The cruel are long hated.
4. Nothing so cruel as a lion.
5. Nothing so fierce as a dog.

SLEEP.

1. He who sleeps little will live long.
2. It is well to rise early.
3. The sorrowful will sleep, but the anxious will not.
4. It is easy to sleep in a perfect skin.
5. To sleep with the turning out of the ox, and to rise with the lark.
6. No good will come from long sleeping.
7. An empty stomach cannot sleep.

8. Ni ddaw da o drachysgu.
9. Ni fawr gwsg un gofalus.
10. Nid cyttun hûn a haint.

CYBYDD-DOD.

1. Amledd cybydd ys tlodi arno.
2. Anhael pob cybydd.
3. Câs dyn y dêl iddo lawer ac ni roddo ddim.

4. Câs dyn a feddianno lawer ac ni roddo ddim.
5. Diawl a leinw uffern â chybyddion.
6. Duw fydd i gybydd ei gôd.
7. Edifar cybydd am draul.
8. Gwae cybydd a gasgl yn amryfflan (yn ddirfawr.)
9. Gwell corawg na chybydd.
10. Gwell cybydd lle y bo na hael lle ni bo.

11. Hir fydd i gybydd ei gabl.
12. Nerth cybydd yn ei ystryw.
13. Ni ludd gyfoeth cybyddiaeth.
14. Nid gwala gan gybydd meddianu y ddaiaren.

15. Nid oes gybydd heb ei lwyth o drallod.

8. No good comes from oversleeping.
9. The anxious will not sleep.
10. Sleep and disease are not accordant.

COVETOUSNESS.

1. The abundance of the miser is poverty to him.
2. Illiberal is every miser.
3. Detestable is he to whom much comes and who gives nothing.
4. Odious is he who possesses much and will give nothing.
5. The devil will fill hell with misers.
6. The god of the miser is his purse.
7. A miser is sorry for the cost.
8. Woe to the miser that hoards much.
9. The lavisher is better than the miser.
10. Better the miser where he is than the liberal where he is not.
11. Long will the miser be slandered.
12. The miser's strength is his craftiness.
13. Wealth will not prevent covetousness.
14. The miser would not have enough if he possessed the world.
15. There is no miser without his load of trouble.

16. Nid sylwyn (llygadwr) ond cybydd.
17. Pan bo marw y cybydd ac nid cynt y ceir lles o hono.

CYDWYBOD.

1. Asgre lân, diogel ei pherchen.
2. Cydwybod yw y nyth lle yr ymddëor pob daioni.
3. Goreu ar bob dyn, cydwybod.
4. Goreu arlwydd, cydwybod.
5. Goreu cyfaill, cydwybod lân.
6. Goreu rhad Duw, cydwybod iach.
7. Nerth gwirgar ei gydwybod.
8. Nid carchar ond cydwybod euog.
9. Nid cydwybod ond llygaid Duw yn enaid dyn.
10. Nid cydwybodus ond cywir.
11. Nid gwybod ond cydwybod dyn ei hun.
12. Nid hawdd cau yn erbyn cydwybod.

CYFEILLGARWCH.

1. A fo gâr iddo ei hun a gaiff pob un arall yn gâr iddo.
2. A gasglo domen a gaiff un câr cywir.

16. There is no pryer like a miser.
17. When the miser dies and no sooner will any good be got out of him.

CONSCIENCE.

1. Safe is the owner of a clear conscience.
2. Conscience is the nest where every good is hatched.
3. The best of every man is his conscience.
4. The best master is conscience.
5. The best friend is a clear conscience.
6. The best blessing of God is a clear conscience.
7. The strengh of the truthful is his conscience.
8. There is no prison like a guilty conscience.
9. There is no conscience but the eye of God in the soul of man.
10. There are none conscientious but the just.
11. There is none that knows but man's own conscience.
12. It is not easy to close against conscience.

FRIENDSHIP.

1. He who is a friend to himself will have the friendship of others.
2. He who gathers a dunghill will have one faithful friend.

3. Bo tynaf y llinyn cyntaf y tyr.
4. Cant câr a fydd i ddyn a chant esgar (gelyn.)
5. Câr cywir, yn yr ing y gwelir.
6. Câr dy gymydog, ond na ro iddo na'th gledd na'th darian.
7. Cywir a dwys fydd câr da.
8. Drych i bawb, ei gymydog.
9. Goreu câr, câr a'm cerydd.
10. Goreu câr, erw o dir.
11. Goreu cyfaill, callineb.
12. Goreu cyfaill, cydwybod lân.
13. Goreu cyfeillach, ymgyfrin a dedwydd.
14. Goreu cymwynas, dangos bai.
15. Goreu cymydog, heddychwr.
16. Goreu cymydog, y callaf.
17. Goreu o'r cymydogion, y difalchaf.
18. Gwell câr cell na châr penill.
19. Gwell câr yn llys nac aur ar fys.
20. Gwell cymydog yn agos na châr yn bell.
21. Gwell gwegil câr na gwyneb estron.
22. Na chais mewn cyfyngder gyfeillach âg ofnog.
23. Na fid dy elyn dy gymydog.
24. Nid anghof brodyrdde (cyfeillgarwch.)
25. Nid câr, ond Duw.
26. Nid cyfaill, ond gwybodaeth.
27. Odid o'r cant cydymaith (h.y., cyfaill cywir.)
28. Rhy dyn a dyr.

3. The tighter the string the sooner will it break.
4. Man has a hundred friends and a hundred enemies.
5. In distress will the faithful friend be seen.
6. Love thy neighbour, but do not give him thy sword or shield.
7. Faithful and sincere will the good friend be.
8. Everyone's mirror is his neighbour.
9. The best friend is one who will rebuke me.
10. The best friend is an acre of land.
11. The best friend is discretion.
12. The best friend is a clear conscience.
13. The best company is with the happy.
14. The best kindness is to point out a fault.
15. The best neighbour is the peacemaker.
16. The best neighbour is the wisest.
17. The best neighbour is the one with the least pride.
18. Better the chamber friend than the song friend.
19. Better a friend at court than gold on the finger.
20. Better a near neighbour than a distant friend.
21. A friend's back is better than a stranger's face.
22. In trouble seek not the friendship of the coward.
23. Do not let an enemy be thy neighbour.
24. Friendship is not to be forgotten.
25. There is no friend like God.
26. There is no friend but knowledge.
27. There is scarcely one true friend out of a hundred.
28. Too tight will break.

CYFIAWNDER.

1. Bywyd cyfiawn, bywyd yn Nuw.
2. Cadarn pob cyfiawn.
3. Call pob cyfiawn.
4. Câs ynad heb gyfiawnder.
5. Goreu tarian, cyfiawnder.
6. Gwell cyfiawnder nag aur mâl.
7. Gwna iawn, ti a gei iawn am dano.
8. Na fo iawn ys pyd.
9. Namyn iawnder ni enwir aes.
10. Nerth brenin, ei gyfiawnder.
11. Nerth cyfiawn, ei gydwybod.
12. Nid cyfiawn ond cariad.
13. Nid cyfiawn ond Duw.
14. Nid cyfiawn ond gwybodaeth.
15. Nid cyfiawnder heb dangnef.
16. Nid oes gan gyfiawnder na golud na thylodi.
17. Nid rhy fynych y gwneir a fo cyfiawn.

JUSTICE.

1. A just life, life in God.
2. Every just is strong.
3. Every just is wise.
4. Odious is a magistrate without justice.
5. The best shield is justice.
6. Better justice than ductile gold.
7. Do that which is just and you shall have justice in return.
8. What is not just is dangerous.
9. Except equity nothing can be called plain.
10. The strength of a king is his justice.
11. The strength of the just is his conscience.
12. There is nothing just but love.
13. There are none just but God.
14. There is nothing just but knowledge.
15. There is no justice without peace.
16. Equity has neither wealth nor poverty.
17. One can too often do that which is just.

CYFOETH.

1. A eirch olud arched i'r cyfoethocaf.
2. A fyno gyfoeth gofyned genad ei wraig.

3. Câs goludog heb haelioni.
4. Cyfoeth a bair falchder.
5. Cyfoeth pob crefft.
6. Cyfoethog pob diddyled.
7. Deuparth golud, boddlondeb.
8. Gnawd i oludog rwgnach.
9. Goreu cyfoeth, boddlondeb.
10. Goreu cyfoeth, doethineb.
11. Goreu cyfoeth, tir.
12. Goreu trysor, daioni.
13. Gwell golud na rhysedd.
14. Gwiw aur i a'i dirper.
15. Ni lwydd golud a wader.
16. Nid cyfoethog ond a'i cymmero.
17. Nid goludog ond diwyd.
18. Nid cyfoeth ond bendith Duw.
19. O gyfoeth y daw gofid.

WEALTH.

1. He who seeks wealth let him ask the wealthiest.
2. He who would have wealth let him ask the consent of his wife.
3. Odious is the wealthy without liberality.
4. Wealth leads to pride.
5. Every trade is wealth.
6. Wealthy is he who owes nothing.
7. Two parts of wealth is contentment.
8. The wealthy are apt to complain.
9. The best wealth is contentment.
10. The best wealth is wisdom.
11. The best wealth is land.
12. The best treasure is goodness.
13. Better are means than superfluity.
14. Gold is proper to such as deserve it.
15. Wealth that is denied will not prosper.
16. None are wealthy but they who enjoy it.
17. There are none wealthy but the diligent.
18. There is no wealth like the blessing of God.
19. From wealth cometh trouble.

CYFRAITH.

1. Anolo (aneffeithiol) yw pob peth ni bo cyfreithiol.
2. Câs cyffredin heb gyfraith.
3. Câs gwlad heb gyfraith.
4. Gwae a ddycco ei henwas i lŷs.
5. Gwell cyduno yn ddrwg nag ymgyfreithio yn dda.
6. Nerth cenedl, cyfraith.
7. Ni ddyly (ni haedda) cyfraith ni's gwnel.
8. Nid cyfraith heb gyfiawnder.

CYFRINACH.

1. Gan rewydd ni phell fydd rhin.
2. Gochel dammegu dy rin.
3. Gwaith celyd celu rhin.
4. Na fid dy wraig dy gyfrin.
5. Nac addef rin i was.
6. Nac addef rin i lafar (siaradus.)
7. Nid cyfrinach ond rhwng dau.

LAW.

1. Ineffectual is everything illegal.
2. Odious is a rabble without law.
3. Odious is a country without law.
4. Woe to him who takes his old servant to court.
5. Better compromise badly than litigate well.
6. The strength of a nation is the law.
7. He has no right to law who observes it not.
8. There is no law without justice.

SECRETS.

1. With the wanton a secret will not be kept long.
2. Beware to allegorize thy secret.
3. It is difficult to keep a secret.
4. Let not thy wife be thy confidant.
5. Tell not thy secret to thy servant.
6. Tell not thy secret to the babbler.
7. It is no secret unless it is between two.

8. Rhin deuddyn cyfrin yw,
　　Rhin tri dyn can' dyn a'i clyw.
9. Rhin elid yn drin (ffrae.)

CYFRWYSDRA.

1. Gŵyr y cadno yn ddigon da,
　　Pa le mae'r gwyddau yn lletya.
2. Ni chlyw Wilcyn beth nis myn.
3. Ni ddelir hên adar âg ûs.
4. Ni ddelir hên geffyl âg ûs.
5. Os nad wyt gryf bydd gyfrwys.

CYHUDDIAD.

1. A ladd a gyhudd.
2. Cyhudda dy hun ac nid arall.
3. Gwell pren cyhuddiad na dyn cyhuddgar.
4. Pan el lladron i ymgyhuddaw y caiff cywiriaid eu da.

8. The secret of two no further will go,
    The secret of three a hundred will know.
9. The secret grows to a quarrel.

CUNNING.

1. The fox knows well,
    Where the geese dwell.
2. Wilkin hears not what he likes not.
3. Old birds are not to be caught with chaff.
4. An old horse is not to be caught with chaff.
5. If thou art not strong be cunning.

ACCUSATION.

1. He that kills will accuse.
2. Accuse thyself and not another.
3. The tree of accusation is better than an accusing person.
4. When thieves accuse each other honest people get their property.

CYNGHOR.

1. A ddwg dda ddrwg gynghor?
2. A fyno gynghor gofyned i'r doethaf.
3. A wreiddio mewn drygioni,
   Anhawdd fydd ei gynghori.
4. Bychan y tâl cynghor gwraig, ond gwae i ŵr nas cymero.
5. Cynghor da ni thyr ben neb.
6. Cynghor hên ni'th addwg (camarwain.)
7. Cynghor ofer un na's ceisier.
8. Ergyd yn llwyn cyssul (cynghor) heb erchi.
9. Gwell cynghor hên na'i faeddu.
10. Gwell bwrw tŷ i lawr heb gynghor na'i adeiladu heb gynghor.
11. Gwna gynghor dy hên gyfaill.
12. Na ymgynghora ond â doeth.
13. Ni châr ffol a'i cynghoro.
14. Ni wnel gynghor ei fam gwnaed gynghor ei lysfam.
15. Nid cynghor ond tâd.
16. Nid drwg dim a wneler drwy gynghor.
17. Ymgynghora â doeth.

ADVICE.

1. Will evil counsel produce good?
2. He who wants advice let him ask the wisest.
3. It is difficult to advise him who is rooted in wickedness.
4. A wife's advice is worth little, but woe to the husband who follows it not.
5. Good advice will break no one's head.
6. The advice of the aged will not mislead thee.
7. Advice not asked for is useless.
8. Advice not asked for is like a shot into a wood.
9. Better to advise the old than to beat him.
10. Better to pull down a house without advice than to erect it without advice.
11. Act upon the advice of an old friend.
12. Do not take counsel except with the wise.
13. The fool loves not those who advise him.
14. He who follows not his mother's advice let him follow his mother-in-law's.
15. There is no counsel like a father's.
16. Nothing is bad that is done through advice.
17. Take counsel with the wise.

CYNNILDEB.

1. A gadwer a geir wrth raid.
2. Bydd di gynnil ar dy geiniog,
    Chwip yr ä, hi ddaw yn ddiog.
3. Cystal y geiniog a gynnilaf a'r geiniog a ennillaf.
4. Da traul ceiniog a weryd traul dwy.

5. Gwell cynnil na chywraint.
6. Gwell toliaw (cynnilo) na heiliaw (gwastraffu.)
7. Haws cadw nag olrhain.
8. Haws toliaw na huriaw.
9. Llunio'r gwadn fel bo'r troed.
10. Mae yn rhy hwyr cynnilo pan eir i waelod y cwd.

11. Ni chadwo yr ychydig ni ddaw fyth i lawer.
12. O geiniog i geiniog fe ä'r arian yn bunt.
13. Oni chedwir y ddimai nid ä hi byth yn geiniog.

14. Tafl â'th unllaw, cais â'th ddwylaw.
15. Yn ngenau'r sach mae cynnilo'r blawd.

THRIFT.

1. What is kept will be had when wanted.
2. Be careful with thy penny,
    It goes swiftly, but comes slowly.
3. The penny I save is as good as the penny I gain.
4. The penny is well spent that saves the spending of two.
5. Better the thrifty than the skilful.
6. Better save than waste.
7. It is easier to keep than to hunt after.
8. It is easier to spare than to hire.
9. To cut the sole according to the foot.
10. It is too late to save when the bottom of the sack is reached.
11. He who keeps not the little will never come to much.
12. By penny and penny the money will reach a pound.
13. Unless the halfpenny is kept it will never become a penny.
14. Throw with one hand, seek with both hands.
15. Thrift begins at the mouth of the sack.

CYWILYDD.

1. Câs a ymffrostio o'i gywilydd ei hun.
2. Hên bechod a wna gywilydd newydd.
3. Na staen cywilydd gwell yw bedd.
4. Ni chyngain (nid cyfaddas) gan genad gywilydd.
5. Nid oes cywilydd rhag gofid.
6. Po fwyaf y câs mwyaf y cywilydd.
7. Yn mhob cêl y mae cywilydd.

CHWAREU.

1. Chwareu ac na friw, cellwair ac na chywilyddia.
2. Chwareu am bob peth ac ymladd am y bwyd.
3. Chwareu hên gi â cholwyn.
4. Chwarëus yn awr, nid chwarëus yn mlwyddyn.
5. Digon yw chwareu rhynawd (ychydig.)
6. Goreu ar bob chwareu ychydigder,

SHAME.

1. Odious is he who boasts of his own shame.
2. An old sin will make new shame.
3. Better the grave than the stain of shame.
4. It suits not a messenger to be bashful.
5. There is no shame against affliction.
6. The greater the hatred the greater the shame.
7. In every concealing there is shame.

PLAY.

1. Play and wound not, jest and shame not.
2. To play for everything and to fight for the food.
3. The play of the old dog and the puppy.
4. Playful now, not playful a year hence.
5. Sufficient is the play of a moment.
6. The best of every play is a little.

7. Goreu yw y gwareu tra ater.
8. Gwell chwareu nac ymladd.
9. Na chwâr hyd niwed.
10. Ni chwery cath dros ei blwydd.
11. Nid chwareu a fo erchyll.
12. Nid chwareu chwareu â thân.
13. Pan fo y gath oddicartref,
    Caiff y llygod le i chwareu.

CHWEDLEUAETH.

1. A ddywed y peth a fyno,
    A glyw y peth nis myno.
2. Anhygoel yw chwedlau.
3. Chwedlau pen gwlad, rhy wir i chwerthin am eu pen.
4. Chwedlau y gwragedd yn y felin.
5. Gnawd i ddyn ofyn chwedlau.
6. Nac adrodd a glywaist rhag ei fod yn gelwyddog.
7. Ni cheiff chwedl nid êl o'i del.
8. Nid mynych gwir oll a glywir.
9. Nid yw chwedl yn colli wrth ei hadrodd.

7. The play is best when left off.
8. Better play than fight.
9. Play not till harm comes.
10. A cat will not play after she is a year old.
11. It is no play that is terrifying.
12. It is no play to play with fire.
13. When the cat is away
    The mice have room to play.

GOSSIP.

1. He who says what he likes,
   Will hear what he does not like.
2. Incredible are stories.
3. The common sayings of the multitude are too true to be laughed at.
4. The gossip of the women at the mill.
5. It is natural for a man to ask for news.
6. Repeat not what you hear, lest it should be false.
7. He gets no news who goes not out of his house.
8. It is not often that all one hears is true.
9. A story loses nothing by being repeated,

DADL.

1. Câs a ddadl yn erbyn pob un.
2. Cymmhwyll (dadleu) ag ynfyd nid gwiw.
3. Dadleu mawr mynych ac egni ar lygoden.

4. Gair mwyn a wna y ddadl yn gadarn.
5. Gair tyner, dadl galed.
6. Haws dadleu o goed nac o gastell.
7. Ni chymmydd dedwydd â dadleu.

DAIONI.

1. A gais a fo da gofyned i'r haelaf.
2. A wnel mâd (daioni) mâd a ddyly.
3. Da dros ddrwg i'r nef a'th ddwg.
4. Dichell ar bob dichell, ymddichellu daioni.
5. Goreu diwedd, diwedd da.
6. Gwna dda dros ddrwg uffern ni'th ddwg.
7. Gwna dda tra bo yr amser yn peri.
8. Gwna ddaioni unwaith ti a'i gwnei eilwaith rhag cywilydd.
9. Haws gwneuthur da na drwg.

ARGUMENT.

1. Hateful is he who argues with everyone.
2. It is useless to argue with a fool.
3. Long and frequent disputing and to be delivered of a mouse.
4. A mild word will make the argument strong.
5. Tender word, hard argument.
6. It is easier to argue from a wood than from a castle.
7. The prudent will not be reconciled to disputes.

GOOD.

1. He who seeks what is good let him ask the most liberal.
2. He who does good deserves good.
3. Good for evil will lead thee to heaven.
4. The art above every art is to be artful in goodness.
5. The best end is a good end.
6. Do good for evil and hell will not have thee.
7. Do good while time permits.
8. Do good once and you will do it a second time for shame.
9. It is easier to do good than evil.

10. Llawer o dda a wna llawer o ddynion.
11. Mawr pob daioni.
12. Ni cheidw Duw rhag neb yr hyn fo dda iddo.

13. Nid da ond Duw.
14. Nid daioni ond o Dduw.
15. Nid rhy awyddus y gwneir daioni.
16. Yn mhob daioni y mae gwobrwy.

DALLINEB.

1. Brenin fydd unllygeidiog yn mysg y deillion.
2. Dall pob anghyfarwydd.
3. Hawdd dal march dall.
4. Nid dall ond na welo ei fai ei hunan.
5. Nid oes neb can ddalled
   A'r neb ni fyno weled.
6. Saith mlynedd y darogenir delli (dallineb.)
7. Wrth ddall ni wiw dal canwyll.

10. Many men can do much good.
11. Great is every goodness.
12. God will not keep from anyone that which is good for him.
13. There is no one good but God.
14. There is no goodness but from God.
15. One cannot be too anxious to do good.
16. In every good there is reward.

BLINDNESS.

1. The one-eyed will be a king amongst the blind.
2. Blind is every unskilful one.
3. It is easy to catch a blind horse.
4. There are none so blind as those who cannot see their own fault.
5. There's none so blind as he,
   Who does not want to see.
6. For seven years will blindness be prognosticated.
7. It is useless to hold a candle to the blind.

DEDWYDDWCH.

1. A fo ysgafn galon ef a gân.
2. Adail dedwydd yn ddiddos.
3. Bid doeth dedwydd, Duw a'i mawr.
4. Cyfoethog pob dedwydd.
5. Diogel pob dedwydd.
6. Duw a leinw ei nefoedd â dedwyddion.
7. Gwell na byd buchedd ddedwydd.
8. Nerth dedwydd, ei amynedd.
9. Ni all drwg ddrygu dedwydd.
10. Ni raid i ddedwydd ond ei eni.
11. Nid aml dedwydd gwr anghelfydd.
12. Nid anedwydd a wnelo arall yn ddedwydd.
13. Nid dedwydd ni ddyffo pwyll.
14. Nid dedwydd ond cydwybodus.
15. Nid dedwydd ond diddrwg.
16. Nid dedwydd ond doeth.
17. Nid dedwydd ond gwybodaeth.
18. Nid dedwyddwch ond pwyllgarwch.
19. Nid goreu gwynfyd yw gallu.

HAPPINESS.

1. The light-hearted will sing.
2. The house of the happy is secure.
3. Let the happy be wise, God will enlarge him.
4. Wealthy are the happy.
5. The happy are safe.
6. God will fill heaven with the happy.
7. Better than the world is a happy life.
8. The strength of the happy is his patience.
9. Evil cannot harm the happy.
10. The happy has but to be born.
11. The unskilful is not often happy.
12. He is not unhappy who makes others happy.
13. He is not happy who has no discretion.
14. There are none happy but the conscientious.
15. There are none happy but the harmless.
16. There are none happy but the wise.
17. There is no happiness but knowledge.
18. There is no happiness but discretion.
19. Power is not the greatest happiness.

20. Nid hapusder ond pwyll ac iechyd.
21. Nid hyfrydwch ond gyda Duw.
22. Nid oes dedwydd heb râd Duw arno.
23. Nid rhaid i ddedwydd nac âch nac eiddo.

DEWISIAD.

1. Câs a gaffo ddewis ac a ddewiso y gwaethaf.
2. Cyfyng ac ëang yw dewis.
3. Dewis ai yr iau ai y fwyall.
4. Dewisaist y gwael yn lle y gwell.
5. Goreu dewis, gwneuthur daioni.
6. Goreu o'r dewis, cyfoeth.
7. Nid dewis ond gallu.
8. Nid dewis ond pwyll.
9. Nid doeth ond dethol y goreu.
10. Tost fydd ar ddyn pan gaffo ei ddewis.
11. Trech rhaid na dewis.
12. Yn mhob dewis y mae cyfyngder.

20. There is no happiness but discretion and health.
21. There is no happiness but with God.
22. There are none happy but have the blessing of God.
23. The happy need neither pedigree nor property.

CHOICE.

1. Odious is he who is allowed to choose and who chooses the worst.
2. Choice is limited and unlimited.
3. Choose either the yoke or the axe.
4. Thou hast chosen the worst instead of the best.
5. The best choice is to do good.
6. The best choice is wealth.
7. There is no choice but wealth.
8. There is no choice but discretion.
9. There is no wisdom but in choosing the best.
10. It is hard on a man when he has to choose.
11. Necessity is stronger than choice.
12. In every choice there is perplexity.

DIAFOL. (Y)

1. A gasgler ar farch malen dan ei dor ydd a.

2. Diawl a bair pob cynddrygedd.
3. Drwg y ceidw y diawl ei wâs.
4. Mae y diawl yn dda tra y sidaner.
5. Myn y diawl y cwbl iddo ei hun fel y cybydd.
6. Ni addawl y diawl y da.
7. Nid da rhodio yn y gwawl lle dalio'r diawl y ganwyll.
8. Rhaid llwy hir i fwytta gyda'r diafol.
9. Soniwch am ddiafol ac fe ymddengys.

DIALEDD.

1. A ddialo air hagr rhoed atteb têg.
2. A fyno ddial yn drwm ar ei elyn ymfuchedded yn lân.
3. Cyn dial gwybydd yr achos.

4. Dialgar pob gelyn.
5. Gnawd dial anghwbl gan anghelfydd.
6. Hwyraf dial, dial Duw.
7. Llwyraf dial, dial Duw.
8. Y neb sydd yn dial ni ŵyr am lonyddwch.

THE DEVIL.

1. What is obtained on the devil's back is spent under his belly.
2. The devil is the cause of every mischief.
3. Badly will the devil keep his servant.
4. The devil is civil as long as he is coaxed.
5. The devil, like the miser, must have all to himself.
6. The devil will not worship the good.
7. It is not good to walk where the devil holds the candle.
8. It needs a long spoon to eat with the devil.
9. Speak of the devil and he will appear.

REVENGE.

1. To revenge a harsh word give a gentle reply.
2. He that would revenge heavily on his foe let him conduct himself uprightly.
3. Before you revenge know the cause.
4. Revengeful is every enemy.
5. Incomplete is the revenge of the unskilful.
6. The latest vengeance is the vengeance of God.
7. The most complete vengeance is the vengeance of God.
8. He who revenges knows nothing of peace.

DINIWEIDRWYDD.

1. A wnelo ei hun yn oen a lyngcir gan y blaidd.
2. Goreu meichiau, diniweidrwydd.
3. Goreu nawdd, diniweidrwydd.
4. Gwirion pawb ar ei air ei hun.
5. Nerth maban, ei ddiniweidrwydd.

DIOGELWCH.

1. Asgre lân diogel ei pherchen.
2. Cystal modfedd a milltir o ddiangc.
3. Gnawd diogelder yn nhrefoed.
4. Gnawd diogelwch am hywil (gwyliadwrus.)
5. Llaw lân diogel ei pherchen.
6. Nid diogel ond a nawdd Duw.
7. Nid diogelwch heb drafferth.
8. Nid gwynfyd heb ddiogelwch.

INNOCENCE.

1. He who makes himself a lamb will be devoured by the wolf.
2. The best surety is innocence.
3. The best protection is innocence.
4. Everyone is innocent according to his own word.
5. The strength of a babe is its innocence.

SAFETY.

1. Safe is the owner of a clear conscience.
2. An inch is as good as a mile to escape.
3. Safety is usual in an inhabited place.
4. The watchful are usually safe.
5. Safe is the owner of a clean hand.
6. He is not safe who is not under the protection of God.
7. There is no safety without trouble.
8. There is no happiness without security.

DIOGI.

1. Aflan dwylaw diawgswrth.
2. Cyfaill blaidd, bugail diog.
3. Differo Duw ddiog.
4. Diog fydd pob ffol.
5. E fynai y gath bysgod ond ni fynai wlychu ei thraed.
6. Gnawd i ddiog gardotta.
7. Gwae a wnel dda i ddiog.
8. Gwae oferwr yn nghynhauaf.
9. Gwr diog,—llawffon y diafol.
10. Hawdd rhifo ysgubau ar faes gwr diog.
11. Hedyn pob drwg yw diogi.
12. Llygad y segur a wêl.
13. Mae anadl y diogi yn mallu pob peth y cwympo arno.
14. Mal y try y ddor ar ei cholyn y try y diog yn ei wely.
15. March i ddiog, ci i lwth.
16. Ni moch wna da dyn segur.
17. Nid diogi ond syrthni.
18. Nid diswrth neb diog.
19. Nid ellir lles o ddiogi.
20. Nid mall tryfall ond diogi.
21. Nid oes ddiogi heb fil o helbulon.
22. Nid ysgar newyn a diogi.

LAZINESS.

1. Polluted are the hands of the sluggish.
2. The friend of the wolf is a lazy shepherd.
3. May God defend the lazy.
4. Every fool is lazy.
5. The cat would have fish but would not wet her feet.
6. It is usual for the lazy to beg.
7. Woe to him who does good to the sluggard.
8. Woe to the idler during harvest.
9. A lazy man is the devil's walking stick.
10. It is easy to count the sheaves on the field of the idler.
11. Laziness is the root of all evil.
12. The eye of the idle will see.
13. The breath of idleness blasts everything it falls on.
14. The lazy turns in bed like the door on its pirot.
15. A horse for the lazy, a dog for the glutton.
16. An idler will not soon do good.
17. The essence of idleness is torpitude.
18. No idler is void of sluggishness.
19. No good can come from idleness.
20. There is no evil thoroughly evil but idleness.
21. There is no idleness without a thousand troubles.
22. Hunger and idleness will not part,

23. Rhaid i segur beth i'w wneuthur.
24. Segurdod a meddwdod a wnant grogyddion yn gyfoethog.
25. Swrth pob diog.
26. Un cam diogi a wna dau a thri.

DIRMYG.

1. Anwir, difenwir ei blant.
2. Câs a ddirmygo Dduw a dyn.
3. Dirmygir ni welir.
4. Gnawd i goeg wawdio ei well.
5. Gnawd i ofer hir anmharch.
6. Gwae a gaffo ddrygair yn ieuanc.
7. Mam fechan a ddifanw plant.
8. Trymaf dial yw dirmyg.

DIWYDRWYDD.

1. A fo ddiwyd ef a weithia.
2. A lafur tra pery'r hâf a gân drwy gydol gauaf,

23. The idle must have something to do.
24. Idleness and drunkeness will make hangmen rich.
25. Every idler is clumsy.
26. One lazy pace will make two and three.

CONTEMPT.

1. The children of the worthless will be disparaged.
2. Odious is he who slighteth God and man.
3. What is not seen will be slighted.
4. It is natural for the vain to scoff their superiors.
5. The vain are long disrespected.
6. Woe to him who gets a bad name in his youth.
7. A little mother will disparage children.
8. The greatest revenge is contempt.

3. Allwedd arian a egyr pob clo.
4. Aml gnoc a dyr y garreg.
5. Deuparth llwyddiant, diwydrwydd.
6. Digon da diwyd genad.
7. Dyfal a dyr y garreg.
8. Gnawd i ddiwydrwydd lwyddo.
9. Goreu celfyddyd, diwydrwydd.
10. Goreu ymarfer, diwydrwydd.
11. Hawdd taflu'r mynydd i'r môr yn ol ei wahanu naill garreg oddiwrth y llall.
12. Maloen a ddyly ei daith.
13. Ni hëuir, ni fedir.
14. Nid difudd y diwyd.
15. Nid oes diwydrwydd heb ar ei ben goron.
16. Nid rhent ond diwydrwydd.
17. O ychydig y daw llawer.
18. Odid difro (alltud) diwyd.
19. Pob yn ddryll yr â'r aing yn y pren.
20. Synwyrol yw yr hwn a gasgl amser hâf.
21. Trech diwydrwydd na golud.
22. Y dafn a dyll y garreg.
23. Y diwyd a gyfyd i radd pendefigion.
24. Ychydig yn aml a wna lawer.
25. Yn mhob diwydrwydd y mae ennill.

3. A silver key will open every lock.
4. Frequent blows will break the stone.
5. Two parts of success is diligence.
6. A messenger is good enough if diligent.
7. The diligent will break the stone.
8. Diligence usually prospers.
9. The best art is diligence.
10. The best practice is diligence.
11. It is easy to throw the mountain into the sea after separating one stone from another.
12. The snail deserves the end of its journey.
13. He who will not sow shall not reap.
14. The diligent is not useless.
15. There is no diligence without a crown on its head.
16. There is no income like industry.
17. From little much will come.
18. The diligent is seldom an exile.
19. Little by little the wedge goes into the timber.
20. Sensible is he who gathers in summer.
21. Mightier is diligence than wealth.
22. The drop will perforate the stone.
23. The diligent will rise to the rank of nobility.
24. A little often will make much.
25. In every diligence there is gain.

DOETHINEB.

1. A elwir yn gall a gais fod yn gall.
2. Bum gall unwaith, hyny oedd llefain pan y'm ganed.
3. Câs anmharchu doethion.
4. Câs brenin heb ddoethineb.
5. Câs doeth heb weithredoedd da.
6. Doeth pawb tra tawo.
7. Doeth pob dyeithr.
8. Doethineb, mal goreuon y mêl, a fydd yn isaf,
9. Goreu doethineb, anwybodaeth am ddrwg.
10. Nid call call wedi colled.
11. Nid call ond a gadwo yn ei gôf.
12. Nid call ond a wrendy gynghor.
13. Nid doeth ond a gais.
14. Nid doeth ond caru gwirionedd.
15. Nid doeth ond cyfiawn.
16. Nid doeth ond Duw.
17. Nid doethineb heb gyfiawnder.
18. Nid doethineb ond gwybodaeth.
19. Nid doethineb ond tewi,

WISDOM.

1. He who is called wise will seek to be wise.
2. I was wise once, that was in crying when I was born.
3. Odious is he who disrespects the wise.
4. Odious is a king without wisdom.
5. Odious is the wise without good works.
6. All are wise while silent.
7. Every stranger is wise.
8. Wisdom, like the best of honey, will be at the bottom.
9. The best wisdom is ignorance of evil.
10. Not discreet the discreet after a loss.
11. No one is wise but he that keeps in memory.
12. No one is wise but he who listens to advice.
13. No one is wise but he that seeks.
14. No one is wise but he who loves truth.
15. There are none wise but the just.
16. There is no one wise but God.
17. There is no wisdom without justice.
18. There is no wisdom but knowledge.
19. There is no wisdom but silence.

20. Nid ef enir pawb yn ddoeth.
21. Nid synhwyrol ond cydwybodus.
22. Pan lithro doeth pob ffol a dery droed arno.
23. Tad doethineb yw côf, a'i fam yw ystyriaeth.
24. Y call a wna ei ran ac a fydd foddlawn.

DRWGDYBIAETH.

1. Drwgdybus, drwg eisys.
2. Drwg ei hun, tebyg arall.
3. Drwg un, drwg arall.
4. Lleidr pob drwgdybus.
5. Mesur pawb wrth ei lathen ei hun.

20. Everyone is not born wise.
21. There are none wise but the conscientious.
22. When the wise slips every fool will have his foot on him.
23. The father of wisdom is memory and his mother is reflection.
24. The wise will do his duty and be satisfied.

SUSPICION.

1. The suspicious is already bad.
2. Evil himself, evil others.
3. Evil one, evil the other.
4. Every suspicious person is a thief.
5. To measure everyone according to his own standard.

DUW.

1. A fedd râd Duw goludog yw.
2. A fo dda gan Dduw ys dir.
3. A fyno Duw a fydd.
4. A fyno Duw derfid.
5. A wnel dyn Duw a'i barn.
6. Cael rhad Duw, cael y cyfan.
7. Cais Dduw yn gâr ac na ofna fâr.
8. Duw a rân yr anwyd fel y rhân y dillad.
9. Golwg Duw ar adyn.
10. Gwell Duw na dim.
11. Heb Dduw heb ddim, Duw a digon.
12. Namyn Duw nid oes dewin.
13. Nid a wna a fyno ond Duw.
14. Nid adwna Duw a wnaeth.
15. Nid agos ond Duw.
16. Nid da ond Duw ei hunan.
17. Nid digon ond Duw.
18. Nid eiddo Duw a wader.
19. Wrth a fyno Duw dim ni ellir.

GOD.

---

1. He who has God's blessing is wealthy indeed.
2. What is good with God is certain.
3. What God wills will be.
4. What God wills let it be done.
5. What man does God will judge.
6. To have God's blessing is to have everything.
7. Seek God for thy friend and fear no ill.
8. God distributes the cold as he distributes the clothes.
9. May the eye of God be on the wretch.
10. Better God than anything.
11. Without God without anything,—God and plenty.
12. Except God no one knows the future.
13. None can do as they like but God.
14. God will not undo what he has done.
15. There is no one near but God.
16. There are none good but God himself.
17. There is no sufficiency but God.
18. It is not the property of God that is disowned.
19. Against what God wills nothing can be done.

DUWIOLDEB.

1. A fo byw yn dduwiol a fydd marw yn ddedwydd.
2. A orchfygo yma a goronir fry.
3. Bach yw crefydd a chwilia beunydd am dano.
4. Crefydd a ladd y drwg, nid yw moes ond ei gadw.
5. Dibech fywyd, gwyn ei fyd.
6. Goreu crefydd, cydymgardodi.
7. Nid diddrwg ond dibechod.
8. Nid llai y crefydd yn unman na'r lle y bo mwyaf y dadleu arno.
9. O ymhewyddu ymhewydd ddwyfoldeb.
10. Ys gwae fro lle ni bo crefydd.
11. Ys gwyn ei fyd gwan ei fywyd.

DYLED.

1. A arbedo ei fach (meichiau) arbeded ei gynogyn (cynddyledwr.
2. Da cael us gan ddrwg-dalwr.
3. Ni cheir gan ddrwg-dalwr ond drwg dafod.
4. Ni thawdd dyled er ei haros.
5. O hir ddyled ni ddylir dim.

GODLINESS.

1. He who lives godly will die happy.
2. He who conquers here will be crowned above.
3. Little is his religion who is daily searching for it.
4. Religion kills evil, morality only hides it.
5. Blessed is he of sinless life.
6. The best religion is to practice mutual charity.
7. No one is harmless but the sinless.
8. There is not less religion anywhere than where there is most disputing about it.
9. If self-devoting, devote thyself to godliness.
10. Woe to the country where there is no religion.
11. Blessed is he who leads a holy life.

DEBT.

1. He that spares his surety let him spare his original debtor.
2. It is well to get chaff from a bad payer.
3. Nothing but bad language from a bad payer.
4. Debt will not melt in waiting for it.
5. From a long debt nothing is due.

DYMUNIAD.

1. Adeiniog pob chwant.
2. ·Adduned herwr hirnos.
3. Bychan teyrnas i chwannog.
4. Dyccid chwant tros peiriant pwyll.
5. Dyn a chwennych, Duw a ran.
6. Gormod awydd a dyr ei wddf.
7. Ni fyn a gaffo nis caiff a ddymuno.

8. Ni wel awyddus ddigon.
9. Nid ei feddwl sydd oreu i ddyn.
10. Po mwyaf gâffoch, mwyaf geisiwch.

DYSTAWRWYDD.

1. Addef yw tewi.
2. Aflafar pob tawedog.
3. Cau dy safn ac agor dy glust a'th lygad.
4. Doeth pob tawgar.
5. Gnawd tawel yn delaid (prydferth.)
6. Goreu doethineb, tewi.
7. Goreu o gampau doethineb, tawedogrwydd.

DESIRE.

1. Every desire has wings.
2. The desire of a fugitive is a long night.
3. A kingdom is small to the ambitious.
4. Desire will entice beyond the bounds of reason.
5. Man desires, God disposes.
6. The too eager will break his neck.
7. He who will not take what he can get shall not have what he wishes.
8. The eager cannot see enough.
9. It is not his desire that is best for man.
10. The more you get the more you want.

SILENCE.

1. Silence is admission.
2. Inarticulate is every silent one.
3. Close thy mouth and open thine ear and eye.
4. Wise is every silent one.
5. It is genial for the silent to be graceful.
6. The best wisdom is silence.
7. The best of the feats of wisdom is silence.

8. Goreu taw, taw·tewi.
9. Gwell tewi na drwg-ddywedyd.
10. Lle taw Duw nid doeth yngan.
11. Nid doethineb ond tewi.
12. Nid tawedog ond goddefus.
13. Po dyfnaf yr afon lleiaf oll ei thrwst.
14. Po gallaf y dyn anamlaf ei eiriau.
15. Taw wrth ynfyd.
16. Tawed doeth, anoeth ni thaw.
17. Tawedigrwydd yw mam pob callineb.
18. Tawedog, tew ei ddrwg.
19. Y doeth ni ddywed a ŵyr.
20. Y tawgar a fernir yn ddoethaf o'r doethion.
21. Yn mhob taw y mae doethineb.
22. Yr hwch a daw a fwytty y soeg.

EDIFEIRWCH.

1. Edifeirwch newydd am hen bechod.
2. Goreu edifeirwch, edifeirwch gwerthu.
3. Mae yn rhy hwyr edifaru ar ol i'r ffagl gynnu.
4. Mor edifar a'r gwr a laddodd ei filgi.

8. The best silence is the silence of silencing.
9. Better to be silent than to speak badly.
10. Where God is silent it is not wise to speak.
11. There is no wisdom like silence.
12. None are silent but the patient.
13. The deeper the river the less noise it makes.
14. The wiser the man the fewer his words.
15. To the fool be silent.
16. Let the wise be silent, the foolish will not.
17. Silence is the mother of every discretion.
18. The reserved is full of mischief.
19. The wise will not say what he knows.
20. The silent will be considered the wisest of the wise.
21. In every silence there is wisdom.
22. The silent sow eats the draff.

REPENTANCE.

1. New remorse for an old sin.
2. The best repentance is repentance for selling.
3. It is too late to repent after the flame is kindled.
4. As rependant as the man who killed his greyhound.

EIDDIGEDD.

1. Anhawdd cydfod eiddigus.
2. Bid ehud drud er chwerthin.
3. Dewin pob eiddig (eiddigus.)
4. Gnawd i eiddigus daraw.
5. Llwm yw grudd dyn eiddigus.
6. Ni hena eiddigedd.

ELUSEN.

1. A rodder i dlawd a delir ddydd brawd.
2. Câs goludog heb elusen.
3. Elusen tam o garw.
4. Goreu aml, aml gardod.
5. Goreu gwaith undydd rhoi bwyd i newynog.
6. Na chais elw o elusendod.
7. Na chryned llaw a rano i reidus.
8. Nid oes dogn ar gardod.
9. Nid oes gwyl rhag elusen.
10. Nid oes rhodd namyn o fodd.

JEALOUSY.

1. It is not easy to live with the jealous.
2. Let the jealous be fickle though he laughs.
3. Every jealous one is a conjuror.
4. It is natural for the jealous to strike.
5. Bare is the cheek of the jealous.
6. Jealousy will not grow old.

CHARITY.

1. What is given to the poor will be paid on the day of doom.
2. Odious are the wealthy without charity.
3. Even a morsel out of a stag is alms.
4. The best frequency is frequent charity.
5. The best day's work is to feed the hungry.
6. Seek not gain from charity.
7. May the hand not tremble that gives to the needy.
8. There is no measure for charity.
9. There is no pretence against charity.
10. There is no gift but through goodwill.

11. Nid rhoddi da a wna dlodedd.
12. Rhodd i dlawd, rhodd i Grist.
13. Tro dy law agored at bob tylodi.

ENLLIB.

1. A ogano a ogenir.
2. Elid gwraig yn ol ei henllib.
3. Enllib ni châr ei enllibio.
4. Hir oreistedd i ogan.
5. Ni fawrheir tra oganer.
6. Ni saif gogan ar gadarn.
7. Rhaid yw genau glân i oganu.

ENWOGRWYDD.

1. A fyno glod bid farw.
2. Dedwydd a gaffo air da.
3. Hwy clod na hoedl.
4. Hwy pery clod na golud.
5. Myfi yn cael yr enw ac eraill yn cael yr ennill.
6. Trengid golud, na threing molud (mawl.)

11. It is not the giving of goods that causes poverty.
12. A gift to the poor is a gift to Christ.
13. Turn thy open hand to all poverty.

SLANDER.

1. He that slanders will be slandered.
2. Let a woman go after her reproach.
3. Scandal likes not to be scandalized.
4. May scandal have a long presiding.
5. It will not be magnified that is disparaged.
6. Slander will not fix on the mighty.
7. One must have a clean mouth to slander.

FAME.

1. He who would have fame let him die.
2. Happy is he who obtains a good name.
3. Fame will last longer than life.
4. Fame will last longer than wealth.
5. I get the name and others the gain.
6. Wealth may perish, fame will not.

ERLEDIGAETH.

1. Diengid gwan, erlid gadarn.
2. Dygas gwaith erlyn.
3. Gnawd i gristion ei erlid.

EUOGRWYDD.

1. Euog a ffy lle nas ymlidier.
2. Gnawd i droseddwr welwi.
3. Gnawd i euog ofn cyfraith.
4. Llais dalen yn y gwynt a darf gydwybod euog.

EWYLLYS.

1. Ceffyl da yw ewyllys.
2. Deuparth rhodd yw ewyllys.
3. Ewyllys heb allu.
4. Heb ewyllys nis gellir ymgais.
5. Lle bo ewyllys bydd gallu.
6. Ni ddiffyg modd pe bae myn.
7. Po fwyaf y gallu lleiaf y bydd ewyllys.

PERSECUTION.

1. Let the weak flee, let the mighty pursue.
2. Pursuit is a hateful task.
3. The Christian is often persecuted.

GUILT.

1. The guilty will flee though not pursued.
2. It is natural for an offender to grow pale.
3. It is natural for the guilty to fear the law.
4. The rustling of a leaf in the wind scares a guilty conscience.

WILL.

1. The will is a good horse.
2. Two-parts of a gift is the will.
3. A will without ability.
4. Without the will there can be no exertion.
5. Where there is the will there will be power.
6. Means fail not where there is a will.
7. The greater the power the less the will.

FFAWD.

1. Ffawd ar ol ffawd a wnant ddyn yn dlawd.
2. Ffawd beunydd ys anffawdd benawr (bob awr.)
3. Ffawd i ddiog nid rhyfaint.
4. Ffawd i ddiriaid ni ryfain.
5. Ffawd pawb yn ei dàl.
6. Gweini ffawd hyd frawd ys dir.
7. Ni bu lanw na bai drai.
8. Ni ludd anmraint ffawd.

FFOEDIGAETH.

1. Diengid gwan, erlid gadarn.
2. Ffo rhag drygdir, ac na ffo rhag drwg arglwydd.
3. Ffoi rhag yr hwrdd i gorlan y defaid.
4. Mae modfedd yn ddigon er diangc.
5. Ni chenir mwyaid ar ffo.

FFYDDLONDEB.

1. Addwyn (ffyddlon) pob meddylgar.
2. Cywir a dwys fydd câr da.

FORTUNE.

1. Fortune after fortune make a man poor.
2. Daily good fortune is hourly misfortune.
3. Good fortune to the idle is not excess.
4. Good fortune to the mischievous will not take effect.
5. Everybody's fortune is in his forehead.
6. Fortune must be followed till doomsday.
7. It never flows but that it ebbs.
8. Want of privilege will not hinder good fortune.

FLIGHT.

1. Let the weak flee, let the mighty pursue.
2. He will flee from bad land that flees not from a bad lord.
3. To flee from the ram to the sheep-fold.
4. An inch is enough to escape.
4. The mass will not be sung on a retreat.

FIDELITY.

1. The thoughtful are faithful.
2. Faithful and sincere will the good friend be.

3. Dedwydd pob ffyddlawn.
4. Gnawd i ffyddlawn ymddiried.
5. Gwell cywir tylawd na thwyllgar cyfoethog.
6. Gwyn ei fyd a fo cywir.
7. Nid anghyfnewidiol ond Duw.
8. Nid cywir ond ci.
9. Nid cywir ond cyfiawn.
10. Nid cywir ond meddylgar.
11. Nid hawdd llygru cywirdeb.
12. Nid hawdd ysgog ffyddlondeb.
13. Nid oes gywir heb iddo ddiogelwch.
14. Y câr cywir yn yr ing y gwelir.

GALAR.

1. A wnêl ddrygwaith a ŵyl am dano.
2. Digon (dichon) Crist trist yn llawen.
3. Gnawd i alarus gwyno.
4. Gnawd i athrist wyraw pen.
5. Goreu galar, galar am bechod.
6. Gwae un dyn a wnêl gant yn drist.

3. Happy are the faithful.
4. It is natural for the faithful to trust.
5. Better the faithful poor than the deceitful rich.
6. Blessed is he who is faithful.
7. There is no one unchangeable but God.
8. The most faithful is a dog.
9. There are none sincere but the just.
10. There are none sincere but the thoughtful.
11. It is not easy to corrupt sincerity.
12. It is not easy to shake fidelity.
13. There are none sincere but that have security.
14. In distress will the faithful friend be seen.

GRIEF.

1. He who does evil shall weep for it.
2. Christ can make the sad joyful.
3. The mournful are apt to complain.
4. The sorrowful are apt to hold down their heads.
5. The best grief is grief for sin.
6. Woe to him who makes a hundred sorrowful.

7. Hawdd peri i fingam wylo.
8. Ni bydd ochenaid heb ei deigryn.
9 Nid trist ond cybydd.
10. Wylid ni wyl ei berchen.
11. Wyneb trist drwg a ery.

GALLU.

1. Eithr gallu nid oes dim.
2. Goreu i bawb a ddichon ei hun.
3. Goreu oll y goreu a ellir.
4. Gwnaed pawb y peth a fedro.
5. Hawdd pob galledig.
6. Heb allu nis gellir ewyllys.
7. Hylaw pob medr.
8. Llwyraf gallu, gallu Duw.
9. Mawr pob medrus.
10. Ni eill neb namyn ei allu.
11. Nid gallu ond Duw.
12. Nid gallu ond gair Duw.

7. It is easy to make the wry-mouthed weep.
8. There will no sigh without its tear.
9. There is no one sad but a miser.
10. Let him weep who sees not his owner.
11. A sad countenance awaits mischief.

POWER.

1. Besides power there is nothing.
2. The best for everyone is what he can do himself.
3. The best of all is what is possible.
4. Let all do what they can.
5. Everything possible is easy.
6. Without power there can be no will.
7. Handy is every skilful.
8. The greatest power is the power of God.
9. Great is every skilful one.
10. No one can do beyond his ability.
11. There is no power but God.
12. There is no power but the word of God.

13. Nid gallu ond gwybod.
14. Nid gallu ond nerth i'w arfer.
15. Po fwyaf y gallu lleiaf y bydd ewyllys.

EDIFEIRWCH.

1. Cant câr a fydd i ddyn a chant esgar (gelyn.)
2. Gelyn i ddyn ei ddamwain.
3. Gnawd i arfawg elynion.
4. Goreu gelyn, a'm ofno.
5. Gwaethaf gelyn, calon ddrwg.
6. Hir y bydd chwerw hên alanas.
7. Ni ludd dysg elyniaeth.
8. Nid gelyn neb ond ei hunan.
9. Pob gelyn heb achos.

GOBAITH.

1. Gobaith gŵr o ryfel, gobaith neb o'i fedd.
2. Gobaith heb gais, mordwy heb long.
3. Goreu gwaith yw gobeithio.
4. Llawer gwaith a ä yn ofer.
5. Nid gobaith ond yn Nuw.
6. Nwyfus pob gobaith.

13. There is no power but knowledge.
14. There is no power but strength to use it.
15. The greater the power the less the will.

ENMITY.

1. Man has a hundred friends and a hundred enemies.
2. Man's enemy is his misfortune.
3. It is natural for the armed to have enemies.
4. The best enemy is the one who fears me.
5. The worst enemy is an evil heart.
6. Long will an old enmity be bitter.
7. Learning will not prevent enmity.
8. There is no enemy but one's self.
9. Every enemy without a cause.

HOPE.

1. There is hope from war, but none from the grave.
2. Hope without exertion is like a voyage without a ship.
3. The best work is hope.
4. Many a hope in vain.
5. There is no hope but in God.
6. All hope is lively.

GOCHELGARWCH.

1. Amgall pob dedwydd.
2. Ar ni ochelo y mwg ni ochel ei ddrwg.
3. Bid wagelawg (gochelgar) lleidr.
4. Gwaith ysgafn ymogelyd.
5. Ni ddaw i neb lwyddiant a fo ry wagelog.
6. Nid gochelgar ond a wylio arno ei hun.

GOLEUNI.

1. Câs tŷ heb olau.
2. Gwell un haul na myrdd o sêr.
3. Nid amlwg ond goleuni.
4. Nid cyflym ond goleuni.
5. Nid goleuni ond deall.
6. Nid goleuni ond Duw.

GORMES.

1. Gormes mawr a dawdd o flaen y glewder bach.
2. Gormes y taiawg ar ei gilydd.
3. Gwan y gormes mwyaf gerbron y glewder lleiaf.
4. Nid hawdd cydymddwyn â gormes.

CAUTIOUSNESS.

1. Cautious is every happy one.
2. Who avoids not the smoke will avoid not its harm.
3. Let a thief be cautious.
4. It is easy to be cautious.
5. Prosperity will not come to him who is too cautious.
6. He is not cautious who avoids not his own desires.

LIGHT.

1. Odious is a house without light.
2. Better one sun than a myriad of stars.
3. There is nothing manifest but light.
4. There is nothing swift but light.
5. There is no light like intellect.
6. There is no light but God.

TYRANNY.

1. Great tyranny melts before a little courage.
2. The tyranny of the clown over his fellow.
3. Feeble is the greatest tyranny in the presence of the smallest courage.
4. It is not easy to bear with tyranny.

GWAITH.

1. Deuparth gwaith ei ddechreu.
2. Goludog pob gweithgar.
3. Goreu gwaith gwneuthur daioni.
4. Gwell gwaith bwa na chryman.
5. Iachaf gwaith, trin y ddaear.
6. Llafur a orfydd ar bob peth.
7. Llawer o waith a wna llawer o ddwylaw.
8. Llwyraf gwaith, gwaith Duw.
9. Mae newid gwaith cystal a gorphwys.
10. Ni châr waith, nis gorddyfno (nas arfero.)
11. Ni cheffir gwaith gŵr gan wâs.

GWALLT.

1. Côchwallt, y gwaethaf o'r holl ddynion.
2. Goreu y gwineuwallt ar bawb.
3. Gwallt du, gwallt dewr.
4. Nid trymach y blewyn llwyd na'r gwyn.
5. O flewyn i flewyn yr â'r pen yn foel.

WORK.

1. Two-parts of work is to begin it.
2. Wealthy every laborious person.
3. The best work is to do good.
4. Better the work of the sickle than the bow.
5. The healthiest work is to till land.
6. Labour will overcome everything.
7. Many hands will do much work.
8. The most thorough work is the work of God.
9. To change work is as good as rest.
10. He loves not work who is not accustomed to it.
11. A man's work cannot be had from a boy.

HAIR.

1. The red-haired are the worst of men.
2. Auburn hair, the best of all.
3. Black hair, bold hair.
4. Grey hair is no heavier than white.
5. Hair by hair the head becomes bald,

CWASTRAFF.

1. A geir yn rhodd a geir yn rhwydd.
2. Afrad pob afraid.
3. Afrad yw gwrthod.
4. Defnyddfawr pob anghelfydd.
5. Gnawd gwedi afrad afrwydd.
6. Gwell ychydig gan rad na llawer gan afrad.

7. Hir y byddis yn llenwi y llestr a ollyngo.
8. Na threulia y geiniog onis ceffych.
9. Sywinaw (gwastraffu) yr arian yn ddim.
10. Yn mhob afrad y mae direidi.

GWENDID.

1. Arglwydd gwan, gwae ei wâs.
2. Fe all diffrwyth (gwan) wneyd ei adwyth.
3. Ni bydd gwan heb ei gadarn.
4. Ni ddichon gwan ond gwaeddi.
5. Trech gwan arglwydd na chadarn wâs,

WASTE.

1. What is received as a gift is easily lost.
2. Everything needless is waste.
3. A refusal is waste.
4. Wasteful are the unskilful.
5. After waste comes misfortune.
6. Better a little with the prosperous than much with the wasteful.
7. It takes a long time to fill a vessel that leaks.
8. Spend not the penny until you get it.
9. To squander money to nothing.
10. In every waste there is wickedness.

WEAKNESS.

1. Woe to the servant of a feeble lord.
2. The feeble can do harm.
3. There is no weak thing without its strength.
4. The weak can only shout.
5. Stronger a weak lord than a powerful servant.

GWENIAETH.

1. Anhawdd i weniaeth dwyllo ond unwaith.
2. Câs wenieithiwr wrth bawb.
3. Mawr gwenwyn y gwenieithus.
4. Na chred i'r neb a'th wenieithio.
5. Nid gwenieithus ond merch.

GWIRIONEDD.

1. A ddywedo pob un gwir yw.
2. A fo hyborth hywir fydd.
3. A fo'n gam ni fyn y gwir.
4. Anferth pob gwir lle nis cerir.
5. Angeu'r euog ydyw'r gwir.
6. Câs gwir heb alw am dano.
7. Câs gwirionedd lle ni charer.
8. Celwydd o ben un, gwir o benau pawb.
9. Doeth pob geirwir.
10. Gan y gwirion y ceir y gwir.
11. Gwell gwir na chelwydd.
12. Gwell un gair gwir na chant gair têg.

FLATTERY.

1. It is difficult for flattery to deceive more than once.
2. Woe to him who flatters everyone.
3. Great is the poison of the flatterer.
4. Believe not the flatterer.
5. There are none so apt to flatter as women.

TRUTH.

1. What everyone says is true.
2. What is in general circulation is apt to be true.
3. He that is false will not receive truth.
4. Monstrous is every truthful where there is no love.
5. Truth is death to the guilty.
6. Odious is truth not called for.
7. Odious is truth where it is not liked.
8. Falsehood from one, truth from the many.
9. Wise are the thoughtful.
10. From the innocent will the truth be obtained.
11. Better truth than falsehood.
12. Better one true word than a hundred fair words.

13. Gwir tros byth yn yr unman.
14. Gwir yw pobpeth ac nid gwir dim.
15. Gwired ys dir yd fain (effeithiol.)
16. Gwirionedd yw mab hynaf Duw.
17. Llawer gwir drwg ei ddwedyd.
18. Llewyrchid gwir yn nhywyll.
19. Myn y gwir ei le.
20. Na chais wir gan ŵr o bell.
21. Nid anhawdd ond cael gwirionedd.
22. Nid gwaeth y gwir er ei chwilio.
23. Nid hawdd amheu gwirionedd.
24. Pawb a geisiant y gwir ac nis gadawant i'r gwir fod yn wir.
25. Rhygas pob rhywir.
26. Taer yw'r gwir am y goleu.
27. Trech gwir na chadarn.
28. Tywyll fydd gau, goleu gwir.
29. Unlliw yw gwirionedd.
30. Y gwir a ddaw yn wir.
31. Y gwir yw cywilydd y gau.

13. The truth for ever in the same place.
14. Everything is true and nothing is true.
15. Truth is sure to have effect.
16. Truth is God's eldest son.
17. Many a truth is bad to tell.
18. Truth shines in the dark.
19. Truth will have its place.
20. Seek not the truth from a stranger.
21. There is nothing difficult but to find the truth.
22. Truth is none the worse for being looked into.
23. It is not easy to doubt truth.
24. All seek truth and will not allow the truth to be true.

25. Extremely offensive is every naked truth.
26. Truth is eager for the light.
27. Truth is stronger than the mighty.
28. Falsehood is dark and truth illumined.
29. Truth is of one colour.
30. Truth will become true.
31. Truth is the shame of the false.

GWROLDEB.

1. Arf glew yn ei galon.
2. Bid drud glew.
3. Caledach glew na maen.
4. Glew a fydd llew hyd yn llwyd.
5. Goreu arf, gwroldeb.
6. Goreu gwroldeb, gochel cynhen.
7. Goreu gwroldeb, ystyr cyn taraw.
8. Gwŷr a wnant gŵr yn wrol.
9. Hawdd annog dewr.
10. Ni ddiffyg arf ar was gwych.
11. Nid calonog ond a gyrcho.
12. Nid dewr ond o wedyd gwirionedd.
13. Nid hawdd ofni glew.
14. Pob ffer dyater heibio.
15. Y dewr a ä yn ei flaen er gwaethaf gelynion.
16. Yn mhob gwlad y megir glew.

COURAGE.

1. The weapon of the brave in his heart.
2. Let the enterprising be bold.
3. The bold man is harder than a stone.
4. A lion is bold until grey.
5. The best weapon is courage.
6. The best courage is to avoid strife.
7. The best courage is to consider before striking.
8. Men will make a man courageous.
9. It is easy to incite the bold.
10. The brave are never at a loss for a weapon.
11. None are courageous but they that attack.
12. There is no courage like speaking the truth.
13. It is not easy to frighten the bold.
14. Every strong one will be allowed to pass.
15. The bold will go on his way in spite of his enemies.
16. In every country a hero is born.

GWYBODAETH.

1. A fyno flaenori boed wybodgar.
2. Braint pob gwybodaeth.
3. Câs nis gwypo ac nis dysgo.
4. Deuparth ffordd ei gwybod.
5. Deuparth gwybod yw deall.
6. Gnawd i brofiadol wybod.
7. Gnawd i wybodaeth draethu.
8. Goreu pob cynnull yw cynnull gwybodaeth.
9. Gwell i blentyn heb ei eni na heb ddysg.
10. Gwell y gŵyr llen na henaint.
11. Heb wybod, heb bwyll.
12. Heb wybod nis gellir gallu.
13. Llwyraf gwybod, gwybod Duw.
14. Ni ŵyr ond a weles.
15. Nid a ŵyr y cyfan ond Duw.
16. Nid byd byd heb wybodaeth.
17. Nid cyfarwydd ond a wypo.
18. Nid gwybod heb weled.
19. Nid hawdd gwybod y cyfan.
20. Nid hysbys ond a ymofyno.
21. Yr hên a ŵyr a'r ieuanc a dybia.

KNOWLEDGE.

1. He who would lead let him love knowledge.
2. All knowledge is a privilege.
3. Odious is he who knows not and learns not.
4. Two parts of a road is to know it.
5. Two parts of knowledge is intellect.
6. The experienced are apt to know.
7. It is natural for knowledge to discourse.
8. The best of all gathering is to gather knowledge.
9. Better for a child if he were not born than to be without knowledge.
10. The learned know better than the aged.
11. Without knowledge—without prudence.
12. Without knowledge there can be no ability.
13. The most thorough knowledge is the knowledge of God.
14. None know but they who have seen.
15. No one knows everything but God.
16. A world is no world without knowledge.
17. None are intelligent but they who know.
18. There is no knowing without seeing.
19. It is not easy to know everything.
20. None know but they who inquire.
21. The old man knows,
    The young suppose.

HAELIONI.

1. A fo hael efe a drugarha.
2. A rano i luaws,
      Rhaned yn hynaws.
3. A ranodd, nef a gefas.
4. A rodder drwy y drws a ddaw yn ol drwy y ffenestr.
5. Câs a roddo o'i eiddo ac a'i gado ei hun heb ddim.
6. Câs llys heb haelioni.
7. Dilyn hael hyd farw.
8. Dilyn hael onid êl yn gi.
9. Gnawd hael ei hir goffa.
10. Goreu haelioni rhoddi cardod.
11. Gwell haelioni na chybyddiaeth.
12. Hael yw Hywel ar bwrs y wlad.
13. Ni ludd tylodi haelioni.
14. Nid ellir hael ar ni bo.
15. Nid hael hael ar fedr cael ced (elw.)
16. Nid haelioni heb gariad.
17. Po haelaf y rhoddwr mwyaf fyth ei enill.
18. Y llaw a rydd a gynnull.

LIBERALITY.

1. He who is liberal will have compassion.
2. He who distributes to the many,
   Let him do it kindly.
3. He who has distributed has obtained heaven.
4. What is given through the door will come back through the window.
5. Odious is he who gives all and leaves himself without anything.
6. Odious is a court without liberality.
7. Following the liberal to death.
8. Following the liberal until he becomes a dog.
9. The liberal are apt to be long remembered.
10. The best liberality is to give alms.
11. Better liberality than covetousness.
12. Howell is generous out of the public purse.
13. Poverty will not prevent liberality.
14. He who has nothing cannot be liberal.
15. He is not liberal who gives with an eye to gain.
16. There is no liberality without love.
17. The more liberal the giver the greater his gain.
18. The hand that gives will gather.

HEDDWCH.

1. Câr heddwch a Duw a'th gâr dithau.
2. Câs cymmydogaeth heb heddwch.
3. Câs gwlad heb heddwch.
4. Diogel pob tangnefgar.
5. Diriaid ni hawddfaidd heddwch.
6. Goreu heddwch, heddwch cydwybod.
7. Goreu heddychydd—gwir.
8. Gwell yr heddwch gwaethaf na'r rhyfel goreu.
9. Ni thangnef gwynnawn â goddaith.
10. Nid tangnef heb Dduw.
11. Nid tangnef ond cariad.
12. Y tangnefgar a gerir gan bob dynion.

PEACE.

1. Love peace and God will love thee.
2. Odious is a neighbourhood without peace.
3. Odious is a country without peace.
4. The peaceful are safe.
5. The mischievous will not be at peace.
6. The best peace is the peace of conscience.
7. The best peacemaker is truth.
8. Better the worst peace than the best war.
9. Dry sticks will not be at peace with the flame.
10. There is no peace without God.
11. There is no peace but love.
12. The peaceable are loved by all men.

HENAINT.

1. A fo hen arched weddi.
2. Bo hynaf y dyn gwaethaf fydd ei bwyll.
3. Can' gwst (clwyf) gan henaint.
4. Goreu ar hen, ei gynghor.
5. Gwae ieuanc a eiddun (a ddymuna) henaint.
6. Hen hawdd gorfod arno.
7. Ig ar blentyn cryfiant, ar henddyn methiant.
8. Nerth hen ei gynghor parod.
9. Ni ddaw henaint ei hunan.
10. Ni ddel oedran i anhael.
11. Ni hena ceudawd (mynwes.)
12. Ni hena meddwl henwr.
13. O bob trwm trymaf henaint.
14. Rhôdd gan hên nag adolwg.
15. Trydydd troed i hên ei ffon.
16. Unwaith yn ddyn a dwywaith yn blentyn.

OLD AGE.

1. He who is old let him ask a prayer.
2. The older a man is, the worse his disposition.
3. Old age has a hundred disorders.
4. The best of the aged is his advice.
5. Woe to the young who desire old age.
6. It is easy to master the old.
7. With a child hiccup is strength, with the old, debility.
8. The strength of the aged is his ready advice.
9. Old age will not come alone.
10. Old age will not come to the illiberal.
11. The bosom will not grow old.
12. The mind of the old will not grow old.
13. Of all pressure the most pressing is old age.
14. Entreat not a gift from the aged.
15. The third foot of the aged is his staff.
16. Once a man, twice a child.

HUNANOLDEB.

1. Am y nofio fo ni waeth ganddo pwy a foddo.
2. Bach pob dyn a dybio ei hun yn fawr.
3. Goreu gan bob dyn ei hunan.
4. Hunanoldeb yw y diafol duaf yn uffern.
5. Nid bach ond a dybio ei hun yn fawr.
6. Y diafol ffolaf yn uffern yw hunandyb.

IECHYD.

1. A eirch iechyd arched i'r meddyg mwyaf.
2. A fyno fod yn iach yfed fêdd (mêdd.)
3. A fyno iechyd bid lawen.
4. Bid lawen iach.
5. Deuparth iechyd, ymrwysiaw (ymarferiad corfforol.)
6. Goreu cyfoeth yw iechyd.
7. Nid cyfoeth ond iechyd.
8. Nid iach ond a fo marw.
9. Nid un anian iach a chlaf,

SELFISHNESS.

1. So long as he swims he cares not who is drowned.
2. Little is everyone who thinks himself great.
3. Every man likes himself best.
4. Selfishness is the blackest devil in hell.
5. There is no one so small as he who thinks himself great.
6. The simplest devil in hell is self-conceit.

HEALTH.

1. He who seeks health let him seek of the greatest doctor.
2. He who would be healthy let him drink mead.
3. He who would be healthy let him be cheerful.
4. Let the healthy be merry.
5. Two parts of health is exercise.
6. The best wealth is health.
7. There is no treasure like health.
8. No one is well but he who is dead.
9. The healthy and the sick are not of the same disposition.

IEUENGTID.

1. A fyno barhau yn hir yn ieuanc aed yn ebrwydd yn hên.
2. Câs ieuanc heb ddysg.
3. Câs ieuanc heb ostyngeiddrwydd.
4. Gwae ieuanc a eiddun henaint.
5. Gwae ieuanc ni wnel gynghor.
6. Hên a ŵyr, ieuanc a dybia.
7. Hên y teimler ergydion a gaed yn ieuanc.
8. Nerth ieuanc, ei ufudd-dod.
9. Nid hudoliaeth ond ieuengtyd.
10. Nid ieuengtyd ond ennyd awr.

LLID.

1. Hwy y pery llid na galar.
2. Hwy y pery llid na golud.
3. Llid ac ynfydrwydd dau enw i'r un diafol.
4. Llid yw mam bradwriaeth.
5. Ni bydd doeth yn hir mewn llid,

YOUTH.

1. He who wishes to be young long let him soon become old.
2. Odious is youth without learning.
3. Odious is a youth without humility.
4. Woe to the young who desire old age.
5. Woe to the young who will not take advice.
6. The aged knows, the young suppose.
7. Blows received in youth are felt in old age.
8. The strength of the young is obedience.
9. The only allurement is youth.
10. Youth is only for the space of an hour.

ANGER.

1. Anger will last longer than grief.
2. Anger will last longer than wealth.
3. Wrath and folly are two names for one devil.
4. Anger is the mother of treachery.
5. The wise are not long angry.

LLWYDDIANT.

1. A fyno lwyddiant gofyned genad y diogi.
2. A lwyddo Duw ni ludd dyn.
3. Anhebyg biau ffyniaw (llwyddiant.)
4. Egni a lwydd.
5. Gwellwell pob ffynedig (llwyddiannus)
6. Llwydd a ddwg lawenydd.
7. Llwyddiant a bair cyfoeth.
8. Ni bydd rwydd (llwyddiant) na bo merth (adfyd)
9. Ni lwydd bendith ni haedder.
10. Nid gelyn ond tra llwyddiant.
11. Yn y lle y bo y da y rhoi'r ac y tycia (y llwydda.)

MEDDIANT.

1. A fo a blawd a gaiff flawd.
2. Arglwydd pawb ar ei eiddo.
3. Goreu bwyall un a bieuffwyf.
4. Goreu enw, mi biau.
5. Goreu o'r adar, a ddaliwyf.

SUCCESS.

1. He who would succeed let him ask the consent of idleness.
2. Whom God prospers man cannot obstruct.
3. It is the most unlikely that prosper.
4. Exertion will succeed.
5. Better and better every prosperous one.
6. Success brings gladness.
7. Success leads to wealth.
8. There is no prosperity without adversity.
9. An undeserved blessing will not prosper.
10. There is no enemy like too much prosperity.
11. Where there is prosperity there will be given and it will prosper.

POSSESSION.

1. He who has flour will get flour.
2. Everyone is lord over his own.
3. The best hatchet is one I own.
4. The best name is, I own it.
5. The best bird is the one I catch.

6. Goreu mantell, un a feddwyf.
7. Goreu rhan o'r deisen a gaffwyf.
8. Gwell aderyn mewn llaw na dau mewn llwyn.
9. Gwell bach a feddwyf na mawr a welwyf.
10. Gwell bach mewn llaw na mawr gerllaw.
11. Gwell bychod (bychan) na chôd wâg.
12. Gwell oen fy hun nag ŷch arall.
13. Gwell penloyn mewn llaw nac hwyad yn yr awyr.
14. Gwell succan meddiant na gwin cardod.

MUDANDOD.

1. Hir y bydd y mud wrth borth y byddar.
2. Mud arynaig (ddychryn) y llafar.
3. Ni roddir gwlad i fud.
4. Y mud a ddywed y gwir.

6. The best cloak is the one I possess.
7. The best of the cake is the portion I get.
8. A bird in hand is better than two in the bush.
9. Better the little I have than the great I behold.
10. Better a little in the hand than much close by.
11. Better a little in the bag than an empty one.
12. Better my own lamb than the ox of another.
13. A titmouse in hand is better than a duck in air.
14. Better is my own small beer than the wine of charity.

DUMBNESS.

1. Long will the dumb be at the gate of the deaf.
2. Mute is the fear of the talkative.
3. A country is not given to the dumb.
4. The dumb will tell the truth.

NATUR.

1. A grïa y frân fawr a grïa y frân fechan.
2. Afel (cyffelyb) pob unnaws.
3. Anian ni ymyrth a'i ymyr.
4. Anifail fydd yr eidion pe torid ei gynffon.
5. Hawdd tynu dannedd blaidd, ond hwyr y tynir o hono ei anian.
6. Naturiaeth pawb a'i dilyn.
7. Nid hawdd newid natur.
8. Nid unfryd ynfyd a chall.
9. Nid ungerdd twrch ac eos.
10. Trech anian nag addysg.
11. Tryw i hwch dyrfu.
12. Yn y croen y ganer y blaidd y bydd marw.

NERTH.

1. Cadernid yw mam pob buddugoliaeth.
2. Ei nerth yw annerth diriad.
3. Nid cadarn ond a fo drech na'i hunan.
4. Nid cadarn ond brodyrdde (cyfeillach.)

NATURE.

1. The cry of the old crow is made by the little crow.
2. Everything of the same nature is alike.
3. Nature will not be repulsive to its cause.
4. The ox is a beast though his tail be cut off.
5. It is easy to draw a wolf's teeth, but it will be long before his nature is taken out of him.
6. Everyone's nature follows him.
7. It is not easy to change nature.
8. Not of the same mind the simple and cunning.
9. Not of the same song the pig and the nightingale.
10. Nature is superior to learning.
11. It is natural for a sow to borrow.
12. In the skin a wolf is born he will die.

STRENGTH.

1. Strength is the mother of every victory.
2. The strength of the mischievous is his weakness.
3. He is not strong who is not stronger than himself.
4. There is nothing so strong as friendship.

5. Nid cadarn ond cyfiawn.
6. Nid cadarn ond diniwaid.
7. Nid cadarn ond Duw.
8. Nid cadarn ond gwybodaeth.
9. Nid cadernid ond anghyfnewidiol.
10. Nid cadernid ond cyfraith.
11. Pob cadarn gwan ei ddiwedd.
12. Sadia'r mur po garwa'r gareg.

NOS.

1. Anaml lles o rodio'r nos.
2. Gadu y nos waethaf yn olaf.
3. Nos a yrr y brain adref.
4. Nos yw mam y cyssulwau.

OERNI.

1. Anghynes pob oer.
2. Nid oer ond y lleuad.
3. Oer pob gwlyb.
4. Rhag anwyd ni weryd canwyll

5. There is nothing strong but justice.
6. There are none so strong as the innocent.
7. There is no one strong but God.
8. There is nothing so mighty as knowledge.
9. There is nothing strong but the unchangeable.
10. There is nothing mighty but law.
11. The end of every mighty one is weak.
12. The rougher the stones the firmer the wall.

NIGHT.

1. Seldom is there any good from wandering at night.
2. To leave the worst night till last.
3. Night sends the crows home.
4. Night is the mother of plots.

COLD.

1. Every cold is uncomfortable.
2. Nothing is so cold as the moon.
3 Cold is every liquid.
4. A candle will not guard against cold.

OFN.

1. Anhyderus pob ofnog.
2. Ergryn llwfr lluaws eiddoed.
3. Gnawd i ofn ddychymmyg ddrwg.
4. Goreu ofn, ofni Duw.
5. Gwan ei galon a gyll, gwnaed oreu gallo.
6. Gwell rhan ofn na rhan cariad.
7. Hawdd yw ofni ofnog.
8. I galon wan da traed buan.
9. Llwfr lladd ei gydymaith.
10. Mae ar lwfr ofn ei lun.
11. Nerth llwfr ei droed hyfrys (buan.)
12. Nid hawdd annog llwfr.
13. Nid ofnawg ond a ffo.
14. Nid llwfr ond a becho.
15. Nid llwfr ond a lecho.
16. Ofna na ofn un gelyn.
17. Ofned pob diofn angeu.
18. Pob llwfr llemitier arno.

FEAR.

1. Every timid one is distrustful.
2. A great many banners will terrify the coward.
3. He who is afraid is apt to imagine evil.
4. The best fear is the fear of God.
5. The faint-hearted will lose, let him do the best he can.
6. Better the share of fear than the share of love.
7. It is easy to frighten the timid.
8. Useful are nimble feet to the faint-hearted.
9. The coward will kill his friend.
10. The coward fears his shadow.
11. The strength of the coward is his swift foot.
12. It is not easy to exhort the coward.
13. None are timid but that run away.
14. There is no coward except he who sins.
15. There is no coward except he who hides.
16. Fear him who fears no enemy.
17. Let every fearless fear death.
18. Every coward will be trampled upon.

PARCH.

1. A fyno barch bid gadarn.
2. A osodo Duw parched dyn.
3. Deuparth parch yw arfer.
4. Diboen i ddyn dybio yn dda.
5. Dyro i'th well ei ragor.
6. Gwell gwr o'i berchi.
7. Na wrthod dy barch pan y cynnygier.
8. Ni chaiff barch ar nis dylo.
9. Parch a'th barcho pwy bynag fo.
10. Parcha bawb a phawb a'th barchant dithau.
11. Parchus pawb a fedd drysor.
12. Y neb na'th barcho na pharch.

PRYDER.

1. A fo pryderus ef a feddylia.
2. Dihunid a brydero.
3. Dolurus calon ofalfawr.

RESPECT.

1. He who would be respected let him be strong.
2. What God appoints let man respect.
3. Two thirds of respect is custom.
4. It is easy for a man to think well.
5. Give to thy superior his pre-eminence.
6. A man is the better for being respected.
7. Refuse not respect when it is offered to thee.
8. He will not be respected who deserves it not.
9. Respect him who respects thee, whoever he is.
10. Respect everyone and everyone will respect thee.
11. Everyone who has a treasure is respected.
12. Respect not him who respects thee not.

ANXIETY.

1. The anxious will think.
2. The anxious are sleepless.
3. Aching is the heart full of care.

4. Gnawd ar eiddil ofalon.
5. Gofal dyn Duw a'i gweryd.
6. Goreu gofal bod yn gyfiawn.
7. Gwell gofal na golaith.
8. Mae gan bawb ei bryder.
9. Po leiaf y gofal mwyaf fydd y llawenydd.

PRYDLONDEB.

1. Goreu cam—y cam cyntaf.
2. Gwell hwyr na hwyrach.
3. Y cyntaf i'r felin gaiff falu.

PWYLL.

1. A fo da ei bwyll a fydd diboen.
2. Ar nid yw pwyll pyd yw.
3. Arf doeth—pwyll, arf ynfyd—dur.

 Cyn dechreu gwel y diwedd.
. Doeth pob pwyllgar.
. Gnawd pwyll yn y bo myfyrgar.
4. Goreu canwyll pwyll i ddyn.

4. Cares are habitual with the feeble.
5. God will do away with the anxiety of man.
6. The best care is to be just.
7. Better care than death.
8. Everyone has his care.
9. The less the care the greater the joy.

PUNCTUALITY.

1. The best step is the first step.
2. Better late than later.
3. The first to the mill shall grind.

PRUDENCE.

1. The discreet is free from pain.
2. If it is not prudence it is danger.
3. Prudence is the weapon of the wise, steel is the weapon of the fool.
4. Before beginning see the end.
5. Every prudent one is wise.
6. There is usually reason where there is reflection.
7. The best candle is prudence.

8. Gweddw pwyll heb amynedd.
9. Gwell hir bwyll na thraha.
10. Gwell pwyll i ddyn nag aur coeth.
11. Heb bwyll heb ddim.
12. Heb bwyll heb ddysg.
13. Meddu pwyll meddu'r cyfan.
14. Ni cheiff bwyll nis pryno.
15. Nid pwyll ond amynedd.
16. Nid pwyll ond deall.
17. Nid pwyll ond gair Duw.
18. Nid pwyll ond ystyriaeth.
19. Tan enw pwyll fe ddaw twyll.
20. Trech pwyll na dichell.
21. Yn araf deg yr ä gwr yn mhell.

RHINWEDD.

1. Gwell rhinwedd cardottyn na mawredd brenin.
2. Nid ä rhinwedd i'r bedd byth.
3. Nid oes dim heb ryw rinwedd arno.
4. Nid rhinwedd ond serch.
5. Rhinwedd yw mam pob dedwyddyd.

8. Reason is destitute without patience.
9. Long consideration is better than violence.
10. Prudence is better than pure gold.
11. Without prudence without anything.
12. Without prudence without learning.
13. To have prudence is to have everything.
14. He shall not have prudence who buys it not.
15. There is no prudence but patience.
16. There is no prudence but understanding.
17. There is no prudence but the word of God.
18. There is no prudence but reflection.
19. Under the name of prudence deceit will come.
20. Prudence is stronger than craftiness.
21. It is slowly that one goes far.

VIRTUE.

1. Better the virtue of the beggar than the dignity of a king.
2. Virtue will never go to the grave.
3. There is nothing without some virtue in it.
4. There is no virtue but love.
5. Virtue is the mother of all happiness,

RHYFEL.

1. Golochwyd diawl annog rhyfel.
2. Mae gobaith gwr o ryfel, nid gobaith neb o'r bedd.
3. Oer yw isgell yr alanas.
4. Yn mhob rhyfel y mae gofal.

TAFOD.

1. Da yw dant i attal tafod.
2. Goreu gwraig, gwraig heb dafod.
3. Goreu o'r gwragedd, y byraf ei thafod.
4. Hir ei dafod byr ei wybod.
5. Nerth gwraig yn ei thafod.
6. Nid o chwai dafod y daw mwyaf doethder.
7. Nid tafod yw llafar câr.
8. Pe dywedai dafod a wypai geudawd ni byddai gymydog neb rai.
9. Tafod a draetha, buchedd a ddengys.
10. Tafod aur yn mhen dedwydd.
11. Tafod têg a ä trwy'r byd.

TRUGAREDD.

1. A gais drugaredd arched i'r mawr trugaraf.
2. A garo fyw'n gyfoethog boed drugarog.

WAR.

1. The religion of the devil is to instigate war.
2. There is hope for a man from war, but not from the grave.
3. Cold is the liquid of the slaughter.
4. In every warfare there is anxiety.

THE TONGUE.

1. Teeth are useful to stop the tongue.
2. The best wife is one without a tongue.
3. The best wife is one with the shortest tongue.
4. He who has a long tongue knows little.
5. The strength of a woman is her tongue.
6. It is not from the ready tongue that most wisdom tongue.
7. The tongue is not the language of a friend.
8. If the tongue told all the bosom knows none would be neighbours.
9. The tongue recites, but the conduct shows.
10. A golden tongue is in the head of the wise.
11. A fair tongue will go through the world.

MERCY.

1. He who seeks mercy let him ask the most merciful.
2. He who would be wealthy let him be merciful.

3. Goreu gweithredon, gweithredon trugaredd.
4. Nerth cryf, ei drugaredd.
5. Nid difalch ond trugarog.
6. Nid trugaredd heb gariad.
7. Nid trugarog ond cydwybodol.
8. Nid trugarog ond deddfawl.

TWYLL.

1. A wnel dwyll ef a dwyllir.
2. Anffawd i'r dyn a'm twyllodd ddwywaith,
    Anffawd i minau o'm twylla y drydedd waith.
3. Anghall mal dall a dwyllir.
4. Antur o dwyll un tro da.
5. Ar ni allo drais, twylled.
6. Call a dwylla, callach a baid.
7. Doeth a dwyllir deirgwaith,
    Ni thwyllir drud ond unwaith.
8. Gnawd i dwyllodrus, ragrith.
9. Gnawd i dwyllodrus wenu.
10. Gwaethaf twyll, twyll ymddiried.
11. Gwell cywir tylawd na thwyllgar cyfoethog.
12. Hawdd twyllo didwyll.
13. Haws twyllo maban na thwyllo gwrachan.
14. Ni hir lwydd a geir o dwyll.
15. Ni thwyllwyd a rybuddiwyd.
16. Nid aur pobpeth melyn.

3. The best deeds are deeds of mercy.
4. The strength of the strong is his mercy.
5. None are void of pride but the merciful.
6. There is no mercy without love.
7. There are none merciful but the conscientious.
8. None are merciful but the moral.

DECEIT.

1. He who deceives shall be deceived.
2. Bad luck to him who has deceived me twice.
    Bad luck to me if he deceives me thrice.
3. The foolish like the blind may be deceived.
4. Seldom does good come from deceit.
5. He who cannot oppress let him deceive.
6. The cunning will deceive, the more cunning will not.
7. The wise will be deceived thrice,
    The bold is ne'er deceived twice.
8. Hypocrisy is natural to the deceitful.
9. The deceitful are apt to smile.
10. The worst deceit is deceit through confidence.
11. Better the faithful poor than the deceitful rich.
12. It is easy to deceive the undeceitful.
13. It is easier to deceive a child than a pigmy.
14. What is obtained through deceit will not prosper long.
15. He is not deceived who has been forewarned.
16. Everything yellow is not gold.

17. Nid hawdd twyllo Duw.
18. Nid twyll ond y byd.
19. Nid twyll twyllo twyllwr.
20. Twyllo arall, twyllo'th hunan.
21. Twyllo arall yn fawr twyllo'th hunan yn fwy.
22. Y somgar (twyllwr) a soma ei hunan yn y diwedd.

TYNGHED.

1. Goreu tynged, diwedd da.
2. Nid eill dyn ochel tynged.
3. Nid i bob aniddawd (amgylchiad) tynged.
4. Nid oes nawdd rhag tynghedfen.
5. Nid twng (tynged) ond a fyno Duw.
6. Trech tynged nac arfaeth.

TYLODI.

1. Anghenawg pob tylawd.
2. Ffol pob tylawd.
3. Nid tylawd ond diog.
4. Nid tylodi ond clefyd,

17. It is not easy to deceive God.
18. There is no deceit like the world.
19. It is no deceit to deceive a deceiver.
20. To deceive another is to deceive thyself.
21. To deceive another much is to deceive another more.
22. The deceitful will at last deceive himself.

FATE.

1. The best fate is a good end.
2. One cannot avoid fate.
3. Fate is not attached to every circumstance.
4. There is no refuge against destiny.
5. There is no destiny but what God allows.
6. Fate is more powerful than resolution.

POVERTY.

1. Needy is every poor person.
2. Every poor person is foolish.
3. None are poor but the lazy.
4. There is no poverty like disease.

5. Tylawd pob grwgnachlyd.
6. Tylawd pawb na wêl eu digon.
7. Tylodi a bair heddwch.
8. Tylodi a bair ymgais.

UFUDD-DOD.

1. A fyno ei garu boed ufudd.
2. Câs gwasanaethydd heb ufudd-dod.
3. Deuparth dedwyddyd—ufudd-dod.
4. Gnawd i ufudd ei hoffi.
5. Nerth estron—ei ufudd-dod.
6. Nerth gwan—ei ufudd-dod.
7. Po ddoethaf y dyn ufuddaf ei gamp.
8. Ufudd-dod i gyfoeth a balchder i dylodi.

UFFERN.

1. Nid anhyfryd ond uffern.
2. Nid eir i annwn ond unwaith.
3. Y cyw a fegir yn uffern yn uffern y myn fod.
4. Ychydig a wneid am y nef pe diffoddid uffern,

5. Poor is every grumbler.
6. Poor are those who are dissatisfied.
7. Poverty leads to peace.
8. Poverty leads to exertion.

HUMILITY.

1. He who would be loved let him be humble.
2. Odious is a servant without humility.
3. Two parts of happiness is humility.
4. It is natural for the humble to be loved.
5. The strength of a stranger is his humility.
6. The strength of the weak is his humility.
7. The wiser the man the more humble he is.
8. Humility to wealth and pride to poverty.

HELL.

1. There is no unpleasant place but hell.
2. There is but one journey to hell.
3. The bird reared in hell will there seek to dwell.
4. Little would be done for heaven if hell were extinguished,

UNDEB.

1. Cadarnach yw yr edau yn gyfrodedd nag yn ungorn.
2. Gwell dau ben nag un.
3. Gwell nerth dwy wrach nag un.
4. Gwell un pen na chan' pen, gwell deuben nag un.
5. Gwell y llysg dau etwyn nac un.
6. Mewn undeb mae nerth.
7. Ni bydd dy-un (unol) dau Gymro.
8. Nid molianus ond cytundeb.
9. Pob undeb a lwydd.
10. Trech dwy wrach nag un.

Y DYFODOL.

1. Da nad pell y rhagwel dyn.
2. Gwr dyeithr yw yfory.
3. I ti heddyw, i bwy yfory?
4. Nid hawdd canfod a fydd.

UNITY.

1. Stronger is the thread twisted than single.
2. Better two heads than one.
3. Better the strength of two hags than one.
4. Better one head than a hundred, better two heads than one.
5. Two brands will burn better than one.
6. In unity there is strength.
7. Two Welshmen will never be unanimous.
8. There is nothing so laudable as unity.
9. Every unity prospers.
10. Two old women are stronger than one.

THE FUTURE.

1. It is well that a man cannot foresee far.
2. Tomorrow is a stranger.
3. Today is thine, whose tomorrow?
4. It is not easy to see what is to come.

Y MISOEDD.

1. Gwell gweled dodi'th fam ar elor
   Na gweled hinon têg yn Ionor.
2. Ionawr a dery i lawr.
3. Chwefror chwyth neidr o'i nyth.
4. Os yn mis Chwefror y tyf y pawr,
   Trwy'r flwyddyn wedyn ni thyf fawr.
5. Cydaid bach o lwch Mawrth a dâl
   Cydaid mawr o lwch y brenin.
6. Mawrth a ladd, Ebrill a flinga.
7. Ni fyn Mawrth waith Chwefror yn tyfu.
8. Os daw Mawrth i fewn fel oen ä allan fel llew.
9. Os Mawrth a ddaw i fewn fel llew ä allan fel oen.
10. Gwlybyn a gwres yn Ebrill a wna
    I'r ffermwr ganu fel yr ëos.
11. Awel oer mis Mai ni wna'r cnydau ddim llai.
12. Blodau cyn Mai goreu na bai.
13. Boreu hir o Fai.
14. Mai gwlybyrog ganddo cair
    Llwyth ar dir o ŷd a gwair.

THE MONTHS.

1. Better see thy mother in her coffin than to see
    Fine weather in January.
2. January strikes down.
3. February blows the snake from its nest.
4. If the grass grows in February it will not grow much
    throughout the year.
5. A small bag of the dust of March, we are told,
    Is worth a large bag of the king's gold.
6. March doth kill, April will flay.
7. March will not have the growth of February.
8. If March comes in like a lamb it will go out like a lion.
9. If March comes in like a lion it will go out like a lamb.
10. If April heat and rain doth bring
    The farmers all do gladly sing.
11. The cold blasts of May make the crops no smaller.
12. Flowers before May had better not have been.
13. A long morning of May.
14. There cometh after a rainy May
    A heavy crop of corn and hay.

15. Mai oer a fydd yn iach ei ddydd
    Yn argoel haf heb fawr yn glaf.
16. Mai oer a wna ysgubor gynhes.
17. Mehefin heulog a wna medel mochddwyrëawg.
18. Mis Mehefin gwych os daw
    Peth yn sych a pheth yn law.
19. Na feia ar dy egin cyn diwedd Mehefin.

Y TYMHORAU.

1. Amser y gwcw yw Ebrill a Mai
   A hanner Mehefin chwi wyddoch bob rhai.
2. Bu lawer gwaith heb auaf, ni bu erioed heb wanwyn.
3. Bu weithiau heb haf, ni bu erioed heb wanwyn.
4. Calanmai mae cyfrif hesbyrniaid.
5. Gauaf glâs wna fynwent frâs.
6. Gwell hanner hâd na hanner hâf.
7. Hâf oer a gauaf cynhes.
8. Hinon heddwch a wna bob tymhor yn hâf.
9. Ni edewis hâf sych newyn erioed ar ei ol.

15. Healthy are the days of May if cold,
    A healthy summer follows too, we are told.
16. A cold May will make a warm barn.
17. A sunny June makes an early reaping.
18. It is well if we can get
    June partly dry and partly wet.
19. Do not find fault with thy shoots before the end of June.

THE SEASONS.

1. The time of the cuckoo is April and May
   And the first half of June, so old people say.
2. Often without winter, but never without spring.
3. Sometimes without summer, but never without spring.
4. May is the time to count young sheep.
5. A green winter will make a thick churchyard.
6. Better half seed than half summer.
7. A cold summer and a warm winter.
8. Fine weather makes every season summer.
9. A dry summer never leaves famine behind it.

Y TYWYDD.

1. Am y tywydd goreu tewi.
2. Ar ol cymmylau yr ä'r wybren yn oleu.
3. Ar ol gwlaw tês a ddaw.
4. Blwyddyn wleb a wna ysgubor lawn, ond nid o ŷd.
5. Dybydd hinon gwedi gwlaw.
6. Enfys brydnawn tegwch a gawn.
7. Enfys y boreu, haul a chawodau.
8. Enfysau ddechreu'r lleuad, gwlaw i'w ddiweddiad.
9. Er maint fo'r dryc-hin, hi ä yn sych-hin.
10. Gnawd yn ol dryc-hin hindda.
11. Gwybren goch y boreu, brithion gawodau.
    Gwybren goch brydnawn, tegwch a gawn.
12. Gwynt o'r dwyrain, gelyn milain.
13. Llif yn afon hinon fydd.
14. Ni thyr gwlaw un asgwrn.
15. Nid y boreu mae canmol diwrnod têg.
16. Niwl y cynhauaf gwasarn gwlaw.
17. Niwl y gaua' arwydd eira.
18. Niwl y gwanwyn gwaeth na gwenwyn.
19. Niwl y gwanwyn gwasarn gwynt.
20. Niwl yr hâf gwasarn tês.

THE WEATHER.

1. It is best to be silent about the weather.
2. After the clouds the sky will clear.
3. After rain comes heat.
4. A wet year will make a full barn, but not of corn.
5. After rain comes fair weather.
6. A rainbow in the evening means fine weather.
7. A rainbow in the morning, sun and showers.
8. Rainbows with the new moon, rain until the end.
9. However great the storm it will at last become fine.
10. After a storm comes fair weather.
11. A red sky in the morning, occasional showers.
    A red sky in the evening, fine weather is ours.
12. The east wind is a bitter foe.
13. A flood in the river means fine weather.
14. Rain breaks no bones.
15. It is not in the morning that a fine day is to be praised.
16. Mist in Autumn is a sign of rain.
17. Mist in winter is a sign of snow.
18. Mist in spring is worse than poison.
19. Mist in spring is a sign of snow.
20. Mist in summer is a sign of heat.

21. Pan goller y gwlaw o'r dwyrain y daw.
22. Pan goller yr hindda o'r gogledd y daw gynta'.
23. Po deccaf y boreu hacraf yr ucher.
24. Tri pheth a gynnydd ar wlaw—
    Gwlydd ac ysgall ac ysgaw.
25. Ucher a ddaw gan ddryc-hin.

YMBORTH.

1. Amheuthyn pob dyeithrfwyd.
2. Bid wyw gŵr heb fagwriaeth.
3. Câs bwyd heb halen.
4. Dewis pawb o'i giniaw.
5. Duw a byrth i fusgrell.
6. Goreu bwyd a heliwyf fy hun.
7. Goreu bwyd, bara.
8. Goreu llaeth, llefrith.
9. Goreu un, diod o ddwfr.
10. Gosymdaith dyn Duw a'i rhan.
11. Gwell mes-saig yn rhad na mêl-saig yn echwyn.
12. Iachaf o fwyd, bara.
13. Iachus arogl bara twymn, afiachus ei fwyta.
14. Llaeth i blentyn, cig i ŵr, cwrw i hên.

21. When rain is lost it will come from the east.
22. When fine weather is lost it will come from the north.
23. The finer the morning the rougher the evening.
24. Three things increase in rain, grass, thistles, and eider.
25. A gloom comes with a storm.

FOOD.

1. Every strange dish is dainty.
2. A man is feeble without nourishment.
3. Odious is food without salt.
4. Everyone has the choice of his meal.
5. God provides for the helpless.
6. The best food is that which I gather myself.
7. The best food is bread.
8. The best milk is sweet milk.
9. The best drink is water.
10. God distributes what is to support man.
11. Better a free repast of acorns than a honey feast on trust.
12. The healthiest food is bread.
13. Warm bread is healthy to smell, but unhealthy to eat.
14. For a child, milk; for a man, meat; for the old, beer.

15. Malldân dan uwd, mellden dan lymru.
16. Melysaf fydd y cîg pan fo nesaf i'r asgwrn.
17. Ni fydd fyw cyw heb aliw.
18. Rhaid i bob cêg gael bwyd.
19. Ydfwyd i ddyn, cigfwyd i gŵn.
20. Yf dy gawl cyn oero.
21. Ys drwg y deg ewin
    Ni bortho i'r un gylfin.

YMDDIDDAN.

1. A ŵyr leiaf a wêd fwyaf.
2. Annoeth llithrig ei dafod.
3. Blaengar ymadrodd ffol.
4. Câs a ddywedo lawer ac ni wrandawo ar neb.
5. Câs a ddywedo lawer ac nis gwrandawo neb.
6. Câs ddyn a ddywedo yn fawr ac a wnelo'n fychan.
7. Dywed llafar ni wypo.
8. Gwell un gair yn mlaen na dau yn ol.
9. Haws dywedyd mynydd na myned drosto.
10. Llawer gair yn wynt a ä heibio.
11. Mae cloch wrth bob daint iddo.
12. Ni chêl ynfyd ei feddwl.
13. Ni ddaw gair drwg yn ol.

15. A slow fire for porridge, a quick fire for flummery.
16. The nearer the meat is to the bone the sweeter it is.
17. A chicken cannot live without aliment.
18. Every mouth must have food.
19. Green food for man, flesh food for dogs.
20. Drink thy soup before it cools.
21. Worthless are the ten fingers that will not bring food to the one mouth.

CONVERSATION.

1. He who knows least will talk most.
2. Foolish is he who has a slippery tongue.
3. Presumptuous is the conversation of the fool.
4. Odious is he who talks much and will not listen to anyone.
5. Odious is he who talks much and whom nobody heeds.
6. Odious is he who talks much and does little.
7. The talkative will say what they do not know.
8. Better one word before than two after.
9. It is easier to say mountain than to climb it.
10. Many a word passes away like the wind.
11. He has a bell to every tooth.
12. The fool cannot conceal his mind.
13. An evil word will not return.

14. Nid â gair i adwedd.
15. Nid mynych gwr mawr ymeiriwr (siariadus.)
16. Nid ymddiddan ond am Dduw.
17. Siarad cymaint a Merddin ar bawl.
18. Un peth yw dweyd, peth arall yw gwneyd.
19. Y doeth ni ddywed a ŵyr.

YMDDIRIEDAETH.

1. Câs a ymddiriedo i rodd.
2. Goreu ymddiried, ymddiried i Dduw.
3. Na chais ymddiried i'r un a'th fygythio.
4. Nag ymddiried i'r glwth am dy giniaw.
5. Nag ymddiried i estron.
6. Nag ymddiried yn fawr i'th elynion.
7. O ymddiried, ymddiried i'th Dduw.

YMRYSON.

1. A ffôl nid doeth ymryson.
2. Ceintach wedi brawd (barn.)
3. Goreu ymryson pwy oreu ei fuchedd.

14. A word spoken cannot be recalled.
15. A great talker is seldom a great man.
16. There is no conversation like that concerning God.
17. To talk as much as Merddin on a pole.
18. It is one thing to say, another to do.
19. The wise will not tell all he knows.

CONFIDENCE.

1. Hateful is he who trusts to a gift.
2. The best trust is trust in God.
3. Confide not in him who threatens thee.
4. Trust not the glutton for thy dinner.
5. Confide not in a stranger.
6. Confide not much in an enemy.
7. If you trust at all trust in God.

STRIFE.

1. It is not wise to contend with the foolish.
2. To quarrel after judgment.
3. The best contention is as to who leads the best life.

4. Gwell taro na lladd.
5. Na chais ymryson â'th well.
6. Nag ymryson âg annysg.
7. Nid doeth a ymryson.
8. Nid gwall synwyr ond ymryson.
9. Pwy bynag sydd heb wraig sydd heb ymryson.
10. Rhwy fu rhyfychawd gynhen.
11. Ychydig yw mam y gynhen.
12. Ymryson â doeth ti a fyddi ddoethach.
13. Ymryson â ffôl ti a fyddi ffôlach.
14. Ymryson â'r gôf yn ei efail.

YNFYDRWYDD.

1. Chwannog annoeth i ymliw (gweled bai.)
2. Gelyn pob ynfyd.
3. Llawer math sydd o'r ynfydrwydd.
4. Llid ac ynfydrwydd dau enw i'r un diafol.
5. Mae llawer gŵydd heblaw yr un sydd yn gwisgo plu.
6. Na fyno weled ei ynfydrwydd heddyw fe a'i teimla yfory.
7. Nid rhaid dodi cloch am fwnwgyl yr ynfyd.
8. Nid ynfydrwydd ond cariad.

4. Better to strike than to kill.
5. Do not seek to contend with thy superior.
6. Contend not with the ignorant.
7. None are wise who contend.
8. There is no want of sense like contention.
9. Whoever is without a wife is without contention.
10. Very little contention is too much.
11. A little is the mother of contention.
12. Dispute with the wise and you will be wiser.
13. Dispute with the fool and you will be more foolish.
14. To contend with the blacksmith in his smithy.

FOLLY.

1. The foolish are inclined to find fault.
2. Every foolish person is an enemy.
3. There are many kinds of folly.
4. Wrath and folly are two names for one devil.
5. There is many a goose besides the one that has feathers.
6. He who will not see his folly to-day will feel it to-morrow.
7. There is no need of a bell for the neck of the fool.
8. There is no folly like love.

CYMHARIAETHAU DIARHEBOL.

1. Can boethed â'r tân.
2. Can chwerwed â'r geri.
3. Can ddued â'r frân.
4. Can falched â chribau y bleiddiau.
5. Can feddwed â'r dwsel.
6. Can felysed â'r mêl.
7. Can goched â'r gwaed.
8. Can gryned â'r bêl.
9. Can iached â'r brithyll.
10. Can loewed â'r dwfr.
11. Can oered â'r iâ.
12. Can wired â'r efengyl.
13. Can wired â'r pader.
14. Can wyned â'r eira.
15. Craffach na'r efail.
16. Cydwymed â'r tês.
17. Crynu fel dail yr aethwyd.
18. Crynu fel y fôrwialen.
19. Cyfreued â phriddell.
20. Cyfrithed â'r neidr.

PROVERBIAL SIMILES.

1. As hot as fire.
2. As bitter as gall.
3. As black as the crow.
4. As proud as the burdock.
5. As drunk as a faucet.
6. As sweet as honey.
7. As red as blood.
8. As round as a ball.
9. As healthy as trout.
10. As clear as water.
11. As cold as ice.
12. As true as the gospel.
13. As true as the Lord's prayer.
14. As white as snow.
15. Surer than the pinchers.
16. As warm as sunshine.
17. To shake like the leaves of aspen wood.
18. Trembling like the sea-girdle.
19. As brittle as pottery.
20. As variegated as an adder.

21. Cyfuwch â'r sêr.
22. Cyffoled â'r cŵn yn cyfarth y sêr.
23. Cysgu fel y pathew.
24. Mal aderyn ar y gainc.
25. Mal baedd yn malu ewyn.
26. Mal bwyd hely.
27. Mal cŵn gan gyfreion.
28. Mal dall yn taflu ei ffon.
29. Mal dau eurych.
30. Mal edyn i walch.
31. Mal eiry Mawrth ar y maen.
32. Mal gwaith Emrys.
33. Mal gŵydd am guddio ei hwyau.
34. Mal llyfu mêl oddiar ddrain.
35. Mal llyn melin ar drai.
36. Mal mant (safn) lleden chwith.
37. Mal myn magawd.
38. Mal rhwymo gwynt yn nghwden.
39. Mal tynu bach trwy goed.
40. Mal ŵy ar drosol.
41. Mal y dur at y pegwn.
42. Mal y garan am ei ddwygoes.
43. Mal y gath am lefrith.
44. Mal y gath am y pysgod.
45. Mal y gwalch dros fin yr ellyn.
46. Mal y llyffant dan yr ôg.
47. Mal y llygoden dan balf y gath.
48. Mal y moch am y ffawydd.
49. Mal y pysg am y dwfr.
50. Mal y rhisg am y pren.

21. As high as the stars.
22. As foolish as the dogs barking at the stars.
23. Sleeping like the dormouse.
24. Like the bird on the spray.
25. Like the boar grinding foam.
26. Like hunting victuals.
27. Like dogs in the couplets.
28. Like the blind throwing his staff.
29. Like two tinkers.
30. Like wings to the hawk.
31. Like the snow of March on a stone.
32. Like the work of Stonehenge.
33. Like a goose for hiding her eggs.
34. Like licking honey off thorns.
35. Like a mill pond on the ebb.
36. Like the mouth of a turbot.
37. Like a kid reared by hand.
38. Like tying wind in a sack.
39. Like drawing a hook through the wood.
40. Like an egg on a lever.
41. Like steel to the pole.
42. Like the heron for his two legs.
43. Like a cat for milk.
44. Like a cat after fish.
45. Like the hawk over the edge of the razor.
46. Like the frog under the harrow.
47. Like a mouse under the cat's paw.
48. Like the swine after the bean-trees.
49. Like fish for water.
50. Like the bark around the tree,

51. Mal y saeth o'r llinyn.
52. Mal y tân yn y carth.
53. Mal y tân yn yr aelwyd.
54. Mal yr ab am ei chenaw.
55. Mal yr eddi am y garfan.
56. Mal yr hydd a'r blaidd.
57. Mor ansefydlog â'r môr.
58. Mor anwadal â'r tywydd.
59. Mor beraidd â'r mill.
60. Mor binc (chwim) â'r pela.
61. Mor ddilês a halen i'r iar.
62. Mor gyfnewidiol â'r gwynt.
63. Mor hylithr â dwfr hyd absant.
64. Mor ysglyfaethus â barcud.
65. Nofio fel y gareg.
66. Yn syth fel saeth.

51. Like the arrow from the string.
52. Like the fire in the hemp.
53. Like the fire in the hearth.
54. Like the ape for her cub.
55. Like the warp on the beam.
56. Like the stag and the wolf.
57. As restless as the sea.
58. As uncertain as the weather.
59. As fragrant as a violet.
60. As brisk as the titmouse.
61. As useless as salt for the hen.
62. As changeable as the wind.
63. As glib as water from the eaves.
64. As rapacious as a kite.
65. To swim like a stone.
66. As straight as an arrow.

INDEX.

	Page.		Page.
Accusation	105	Cunning	105
Adversity	7	Deafness	73
Advice	107	Death	31
Agreement	25	Debt	139
Agriculture	21	Deceit	201
Anger	181	Desire	141
Anxiety	193	Devil, The	123
Argument	115	Diligence	129
Blindness	117	Dishonesty	51
Borrowing	69	Dumbness	185
Cautiousness	159	Education	13
Charity	145	Enmity	157
Choice	121	Envy	85
Cold	189	Failure	19
Complaint	7	Falsehood	55
Confidence	219	Fame	147
Conscience	95	Fate	203
Contempt	129	Fault	63
Contentment	69	Fear	191
Conversation	217	Fidelity	151
Courage	169	Flattery	165
Covetousness	93	Flight	151
Credulity	89	Folly	221
Cruelty	91	Food	215

INDEX.

	Page.		Page.
Forgetfulness	39	Mercy	199
Fortune	151	Misfortune	29
Friendship	95	Money	61
Future, The	207	Months, The	209
God	137	Music	85
Godliness	139	Nature	187
Good	115	Necessity	35
Gossip	113	Night	189
Grief	153	Old Age	177
Guilt	149	Patience	27
Hair	161	Peace	175
Happiness	119	Perjury	55
Haste	71	Persecution	149
Hatred	83	Play	111
Health	179	Possession	183
Hell	205	Poverty	203
Home	81	Power	155
Honour	53	Practice	59
Hope	157	Praise	75
Humility	205	Pride	65
Ignorance	57	Promise	9
Inconsistency	41	Protection	25
Independence	45	Prudence	195
Innocence	125	Punctuality	195
Intemperance	39	Punishment	89
Jealousy	145	Rebuke	87
Jokes	83	Repentance	143
Judgment	67	Respect	193
Justice	99	Revenge	123
Kindness	77	Safety	125
Knowledge	171	Seasons, The	211
Law	103	Secrets	103
Laziness	127	Selfishness	179
Liberality	173	Shame	111
Life	73	Sickness	17
Light	159	Silence	141
Love	77	Similes, Proverbial	223
Meekness	11	Slander	147
Memory	87	Sleep	91

Lightning Source UK Ltd.
Milton Keynes UK
UKOW05f1816310517
302413UK00004B/418/P